The Things I Have Seen and Heard

Sharon Shemwell

Copyright 2017 by Sharon Shemwell.
The book author retains sole copyright to
her contributions to this book.

Published 2017.

Printed in the United States of America.

All rights reserved.

No portion of this book may be reproduced, stored in a retrieval system, or transmitted in any form or by any means – electronic, mechanical, photocopy, recording, scanning, or other – except for brief quotations in critical reviews or articles, without the prior written permission of the author.

ISBN 978-1-943650-65-1

Published by BookCrafters, Parker, Colorado.
www.bookcrafters.net

Foreword

I count it a privilege and such an honor to be asked to write the forward of this book of testimonies entitled "The Things I Have Seen and Heard." The title reminds me of Acts chapter 4, where a notable miracle had occurred. The healing of the lame man by Peter and John had stirred the community, and the religious council could not deny the power of God. After much discussion and deliberation, the council threatened the Apostles not to "teach or speak in the Name of Jesus again."

But Peter and John answered and said unto them, "Whether it be right in the sight of God to hearken unto you more than unto God, judge ye. For we cannot but speak the things which we have seen and heard." (Acts 4:19-20) What a powerful statement, and how true are "the things I have seen and heard!"

There is something about a testimony that is very powerful. As a Christian begins to tell the things that God has done, it is health to the hearer. Testimonies are so important in the day in which we live. Because most people focus on the negative, we must tell how God has helped and strengthened us.

Powderly Holiness Church is celebrating 50 years—a Jubilee! I thought if only the walls could talk. But, of course, they can't. Therefore, you must tell what you have seen and heard.

The following pages hold a small account of the mighty miracles God has wrought in this church for over half a century. For the past 50 years, the church has seen growth spiritually and in numbers. There have been building projects, upgrades, and many positive changes. My! How the Lord has increased and blessed!

The church is also celebrating Brother Larry Shemwell's 40 years as pastor. Once again, I can only tell you the things I have seen and heard. Brother Shemwell seeks no glory or admiration; he is a very humble man. He is a true shepherd of the flock of God, always showing concern and consideration for his congregation. The times the Elder has addressed the congregation, while I was visiting, I have seen love in his eyes. I believe he loves and has compassion just like Jesus.

Elder Shemwell is a unique individual—always bringing a fresh look to difficult issues in the Scriptures. I can honestly say that he is a friend. The Bible says, "A friend loveth at all times." Larry Shemwell fits that description. During very hard trials in my life, Brother Shemwell has shown me love and been an anchor for me. He, of course, has told me when I was wrong; but not without the love of Christ. One principle he taught me was: "Where there is NO WOOD, the fire goes out." I wish I had learned that years ago. Another way to say it is: "Learn to shut up, Brother Drew."

I am very thankful I was introduced to the Powderly Holiness Church many years ago. I have seen and heard so many wonderful things that the Lord has done. As you read these testimonies about the power of God, allow them to increase your faith and cause you to become an overcomer. I can say, "I am a better person because of the friendship of the saints of Powderly Holiness Church and Pastor Larry Shemwell."

I have lifetime friends that I will cherish, and someday, we will spend eternity together dancing around the THRONE...that's a Powderly thing...like y'all dancing around the Bible stand....God bless each and every one of you as you continue in HIS service.

Reverend Charles Drew

Introduction

The last 50 years have sped by. It seems like only yesterday that I was just a young boy lying under the pew. I vividly remember feeling the power of the Holy Ghost as it swept through the church as the saints of God worshiped the Lord.

From the Sunday afternoon services to radio broadcasts live from the church to tent revivals—God has surely been among the folks at Powderly Holiness Church.

I feel humbled to have had the privilege to pastor such a great flock of sheep. I have been very blessed is the only way I can describe it.

Sister Tilda and I, along with the entire congregation, appreciate everything that has been done to make this Jubilee Celebration such a success. Special thank you goes to Sister Sharon Shemwell, Sister Diane Mouser, Sister Kimberly Wilson, and Sister Penny Saylor for coordinating this event. Thanks goes to Sister Sharon Shemwell for putting this book together to preserve our legacy for the future generations. A special thank you goes to Brother Joshua Shemwell for helping to edit this book and taking care of getting the photos ready for submission. I also want to thank Greg Lamb, owner of Studio III, for taking the cover photo. But let it be known, it would have been impossible without the help and assistance of those in the congregation that pulled together to make this a memorable occasion.

I was able to personally witness or be a part of many of the miracles and answered prayers that you will read about in this book. Get comfortable, take your time, and stroll down memory lane with me for a while.

Brother Larry and Sister Tilda Shemwell
Pastor and First Lady of Powderly Holiness Church

BROTHER LARRY AND SISTER TILDA SHEMWELL

Virginia

The Flener home changed forever on January 10, 1916. They welcomed their brand-new baby girl---Virginia Lucille in Butler County, Kentucky. She was a happy baby and a helpful young girl. While still at home, her mother Vuna took her along to the neighbors' houses as she helped in the delivery of their babies. Vuna never claimed to be a midwife. That was just how things were done back then. She never knew at the time that she was preparing Virginia for a God-given calling in her life. Virginia never kept count of how many babies she delivered in her lifetime, but she delivered most of her grandchildren and plenty of her great-grandchildren. She was also there for the members of other churches and anyone that needed her.

    She and her sister-in-law Edith Flener made a great team. Whenever they received a call, the family was left behind to fend for themselves as they went to help. Sometimes they would be gone for many days. It wasn't like they had nothing else to do. Virginia herself had a family of 15 children; while Edith had a family of 8 children.

They practiced the lyrics to an old song that Virginia sang many times in church services.

"Old-Fashion Love"

"Give me that old-fashion love like they had long ago.
Way back when the old folks were young.
A friend in need was a friend indeed,
Help me that, dear Lord to be.
That old-fashion love just can't be beat.

When the old folks were young, they had that great love.
They'd go for many miles around.
There to help in their need and to cheer them in their grief.
And when they prayed, the power of God came down."

About 2 weeks after her 82nd birthday, she delivered her last baby on January 29, 1998. It was her great-grandson Kolton Blake Drake.

VIRGINIA AND EDITH FLENER TAKEN AT THE DELIVERY OF SHANNON SHEMWELL 03/22/1977

The Conversion

Virginia was reared during the time of the Great Depression in America, which explains her very conservative lifestyle. She lived a very simple life and could stretch a dollar until it begged for mercy or pinch a penny until Lincoln cried out. She and her siblings were hungry many times growing up, so she never wanted to waste anything. She could whip up a delicious meal out of nearly nothing. I give her credit for being one of the most outstanding culinary chefs with no formal training. She has had the privilege of feeding hundreds of people during her time on earth. She was a great hostess and provided housing to anyone in need. Folks would come and stay for months or even years at a time.

Everyone called her "Peggy" or "Grandmother." She never liked the name Virginia, because she was afraid of growing up and being called Aunt Ginny. She unofficially changed her name to "Peggy." When the grandchildren came along, they began calling her Grandmother. A few called her Mama Peggy.

Vuna (I will call her Mammy for the duration of the book. That's what she was called by her grandchildren.) and her children moved to Muhlenberg County, Kentucky, when Peggy was a girl. Vuna belonged to the Church of Christ faith. There were no holiness or Apostolic churches available to attend in Muhlenberg County when Peggy was a child.

One year while Peggy was a young girl, Brother Jim Smith, a holiness preacher, held a Gospel meeting in the Central City Park. She and her mother attended. Mammy told Peggy when they arrived back home, "I don't understand what that man was preaching, but it was the truth."

She also gave Peggy a warning concerning those holiness preachers that preached about baptism in the Name of Jesus Christ, "If I ever catch you on that mourner's bench (altar), I will drag you off by the hair of your head."

As Peggy listened to Brother Jim Smith preach that year, it ignited a fire in her soul---a hunger to hear more about this holiness way. But she was not privileged to attend church or hear inspiring sermons on a regular basis.

PEGGY AND HER FAMILY HERE
L-R: BROTHER GILMON, MOTHER (VUNA), PEGGY,
FRONT ROW: SISTER AILENE

Starting a Home

Wilbur Shemwell was born in Muhlenberg County, Kentucky, on July 2, 1912. I'm not sure of the details of how Wilbur and Peggy met, but I can say the Divine Providence of God brought them together. Had it not been for these two individuals, there would have been no Powderly Holiness Church.

They were married on August 8, 1934.

As they began their new life together, Peggy never forgot the hunger for God she had felt as a young girl. God allowed her to have a neighbor, a backslidden woman, that began to share with her the plan of Salvation. She enlightened her on the necessity of being baptized in Jesus' Name. Peggy began attending some house services and any place she could find where services were being held. They owned very few automobiles, so most of the time she had to walk or hitch a ride.

What a joy when she repented of her sins and was baptized in Jesus' Name in November 1935! It totally consumed her and made a new creature out of her. Mammy and Wilbur were not so happy about this new person and attempted to make things miserable for her. Wilbur tried to hinder her from attending church. Mammy told her they would cast some kind of spell on her. Nevertheless, she loved her Jesus more than anything in the world!

Wilbur loved to go to the movie house. He would take Peggy by the church and leave her; then go out for the night. When he finished, he expected her to be ready to go. Of course, with no air conditioning during those days, he would stand at the open back door. When she looked his way, he would motion for her to leave. She got wise to his ways and would not look back; then she wouldn't have to leave. One night he stuck his head inside, trying to get her attention. A sister in the church was under the influence of the Spirit and dancing and worshiping the Lord. As Wilbur stuck his head inside, her arm swung out and hit him in the eye. He went home that night with a BLACK eye.

He began to get more and more intolerable to live with. He would forbid Peggy to go to church. She was trying to be a Christian and would stay home; but not without praying and giving Wilbur to God. She would have his evening meal on the table when he arrived home in the afternoons. No place setting for her, because she was "pushing her plate back" (fasting). He would get so angry because she was not eating, and he would shake the entire table and rattle the dishes. Peggy just continued to obey God by prayer and fasting. God began to place Wilbur under conviction. Prior to this time, he feared NOTHING. He would hear noises in the attic and under the bed at night. He got to where he couldn't even sleep. But it all paid off when Wilbur bowed his knee in repentance and surrendered to God. Things began to return to harmony in the Shemwell household. But Mammy was not a happy camper. God later called Wilbur to be a holiness preacher.

Children began to come along. The first child born to Wilbur and Peggy was a little girl named Esther Pearl. She developed some problems and died in infancy. Peggy thought she would never be able to have any more children. Little did she know, she would have an additional 8 daughters and 6 sons: Euphrada Joyce, June Vondell, Shirley Jelane, Beverly Sharron, Larry Wilbur, Patricia Gayle, Lonnie Wayne, Ronnie Dwayne, Rebecca Diann, Deborah Jean, Vickie Karen, Keith Doyle, Dennis Marlow, and Kevin Allen.

WILBUR & PEGGY

FAMILY PICTURE TAKEN IN 1975

A New Life

As Peggy heard about the Holy Ghost, she desired it more than anything in this world. She would go throughout her day, and squat here and pray, and squat there and pray. She thought about Jesus all day long. Although she had heard about the Holy Ghost, she had never personally witnessed anyone receiving it and didn't know what to expect. One night after retiring for the night, she began to talk to God. As she did, she began to laugh. She quenched the Spirit; because she thought, "It sure doesn't come that way."

She also felt the quickening Spirit at one point and thought the same thing.

Sometime later, she attended a house service. Joyce was her baby. As service was going on, she wanted to get involved; but Joyce was being very fussy that night. She tried laying her on the bed, but Joyce would not lie there. She just wanted to spank her. But something inside spoke to her and said, "In your patience possess ye your soul." Instead, she just tried to console Joyce.

A lady testified as the service went on and said, "In the day you give God your whole heart, He will be found of you."

She didn't particularly like this lady and had been harboring a grudge about something. But when she heard those words, she looked up to heaven and said in her mind, "God, as much as I know how, here is my whole heart."

Something that felt like a bolt of lightning hit her in the top of her head and knocked her to the floor. The next thing she knew, she came to herself and heard herself laughing hysterically. She would laugh awhile and speak in tongues awhile. She tried getting up several different times and wasn't able. She went home that night with "joy unspeakable and full of glory!"

WILBUR, PEGGY, AND BABY

Wilbur evangelized for many years, often traveling alone, while Peggy stayed behind to care for the home and children. Money was scarce; times were hard. It was often difficult to find resources to feed and clothe the children and to keep the house warm. One summer, they survived on okra and potatoes; potatoes and okra. Yet God never forsook them. He doesn't always supply our wants, but He does supply our needs.

One time in particular, a bill was due. There were no government assistance programs available. You had to trust God. Mammy gave them a piece of property near her home in Central City. They built a home on the property. The upstairs was unfinished. Sister Shemwell went upstairs on one of the floor joists (She always called it the "plank" when testifying about it.) to pray and entreat God. All of a sudden, she felt a "tinge" from heaven and knew everything was going to be okay. All throughout the day, the Devil reminded her that she still did not have the money. Nevertheless, she kept praising the Lord for it. About 4:00 that afternoon, someone knocked on the door and brought her the exact amount of money that she needed to pay the bill. God does care about His own!

Wilbur

Brother Shemwell preached very often in Hammond, Indiana; Chicago, Illinois; Tellahoma, Tennessee; and Bridgeman, Michigan.

He sang a song called "Ananias," when he would visit different churches. The people in Hammond, Indiana, in particular, began to call him by that name.

"Ananias"

"Ananias, tell me what kind of man Jesus is.
Oh, Ananias, oh, Ananias, just tell me what kind of man Jesus is.
Well, He spoke to the cripple and the cripple man walked.
Tell me what kind of man Jesus is.
Oh Ananias, oh, Ananias, tell me what kind of man Jesus is."

The song had several additional verses. This just gives you an idea of how it went.

Brother Shemwell preached several times on Maxwell Street in Chicago, Illinois. This was known for its drunken derelicts. As he was preaching on the street corner during one visit, a drunk came along asking for something to eat. Brother Shemwell noticed a man with a hot dog cart nearby and offered to buy the drunk something to eat. The owner of the cart said, "He doesn't want anything to eat. He just wants your money."

Brother Shemwell informed him to feed the man as many hot dogs as he wanted. He said, "When he is done, I will pay you." I can still hear him tell this testimony after all those years. He said, "That man ate TWELVE hot dogs."

He wasn't concerned about preaching in the nicest cathedrals. There were many times when he told the churches to keep their money. He wasn't preaching for wealth or fame; but, rather, to win a soul to Christ.

He sang another song that he is still remembered for.

> "I don't want your worldly pleasures.
> I don't want your silver and gold.
> All I want is the love of Jesus
> For to save my dying soul.
>
> God is God and there's no other
> Who can heal the sick and lame
> But remember, everybody
> It must be done in Jesus' Name.
>
> God is God and there's no other
> Who can save the soul of man
> Jesus said to Nicodemus
> Oh, ye must be born again."

During his early years of living for God, he was on his way to Hartford, Kentucky, to church with Brother Jim Smith and his wife. They stopped at a service station in Central City to get gas (where the Brother's BBQ is currently located). There were no self-service stations. Brother Smith told the attendant, "Fill it up." Times were hard. Money was scarce. Brother Smith waited outside the car while it was being filled with gas. He just walked around whistling.

Sister Smith and Brother Shemwell were inside the car. She looked at Brother Shemwell and said, "Do you have any money?"

He replied, "No."

She said, "Neither does he."

Right before the pump clicked off, someone came walking down the street. They hollered at Brother Smith and said, "Brother Jim, don't you pay for that. I'm going to."

He began to dance and praise God all over that parking lot!

When the draft began for World War II, Wilbur received a letter that he was being drafted. He felt like he could not join the armed forces and please God. They sent him to Owensboro, Kentucky, to appear before the federal board to explain his reason for not being able to go.

Brother Will Johnson had already been jailed for his refusal and received the Holy Ghost while incarcerated.

When Wilbur appeared before the elite personnel, they began to question him. As he answered their questions, they told him, "If we believed like you, we wouldn't win this war."

He replied, "No, if you believed like me, there wouldn't be any war."

Needless to say, he was never called. God fought the battle for him.

A lady attended one of the church services during the 1970s. She had a large goiter on her neck that was very visible. During the course of the service, she stood up and said, "Brother Wilbur, God told you to pray for me and He would heal me."

Sure enough, God had already spoken to Brother Shemwell. Immediately, he went and laid hands on her and began to pray. God instantly removed the goiter and she went home totally healed!

The Church

Brother Shemwell inquired about renting the first church building about 1967. It was a 20x25 wood-frame building. The building was definitely nothing fancy—just a place to worship God. When he contacted the owners, they first said no; but then one of them felt like they should rent it to him. It was plain and simple, but the Spirit of God was there. It would be packed out most services and even have people gathered in the parking lot. Then there were times things would be slim. Brother Shemwell would do without for the work of God. He was never one that had dollar signs in his eyes. He was just an old-time preacher man.

For a little while, the congregation moved to Browder. Brother Lester Stevens pastored in Russellville, Kentucky. He had a building in Browder that he rented to Brother Shemwell. The Lord moved there, but things just didn't seem right. The congregation eventually ended up back in Powderly.

Brother Shemwell came back to Powderly and purchased the church. The first church sat upon the hill right off Highway 62. This was before the 4-lane was built that runs in front of the church today. At one time, we had a Kingdom Hall (Jehovah Witness church) below the hill in front of us. We eventually added a 10-foot platform to the church and Sunday School rooms down one side.

Sister Shemwell always said, "When Wilbur makes up his mind, he can touch God and get things done."

In 1978, Larry asked his Dad to go with him to take a look at the condition of the building. It was literally falling down—deteriorating before our very eyes. The top looked like a sway-backed mule! We ended up tearing it down with the exception of one wall and the floor. In the meantime, we began having church services in a garage that was located next door to Elder Shemwell's house. We actually turned the sanctuary around as we rebuilt the church to make it wider, now having three rows of pews instead of two.

We stayed in that church until 1984 and made plans to build a new sanctuary. We had outgrown the second church as membership grew and babies were being born. We purchased the old Kingdom Hall building to use for part of our Christian school. We moved the wood-frame building down the hill and began a new phase of construction. We moved into this building in the spring of 1985. Elder Shemwell was able to enjoy the new building before God called him home.

We continued to grow in membership and were experiencing growing pains again in 2006. We started construction on a new sanctuary and moved in during the spring of 2007. We are only enjoying the fruits of the elders that have gone on before us.

FIRST CHURCH
THIS WAS THE INTERIOR OF THE ORIGINAL CHURCH BUILDING.
IT WAS NOT MUCH WIDER THAN THIS.
PICTURE JUST GIVES YOU AN IDEA OF ITS SIZE.
L-R: Tony Daniel, Marty Shemwell, Wilbur Shemwell, Ronnie Shemwell, Sharon Shemwell, Keith Shemwell, Lonnie Shemwell, Peggy Shemwell, Larry Shemwell, AND Kevin Shemwell

2ND CHURCH BEFORE IT WAS RAZED

CONSTRUCTION OF 3RD SANCTUARY BEGAN IN 1984.
WE MOVED INTO THE BUILDING IN 1985.

THIRD SANCTUARY IS PRESENT DAY FELLOWSHIP HALL

CONTRUCTION AND COMPLETION OF 4TH SANCTUARY

BROTHER HENRY TRAVIS
LAYING BLOCKS

TONY DANIEL AND
KEITH SHEMWELL

GROUP OF MEN WORKING ON SUB-FLOORING

SHAWN SIGERS

JOSHUA, LARRY, KEITH SHEMWELL

RAISING THE WALL

LARRY SHEMWELL

CRANE AND TRUSS

FINISHED BUILDING

Church Dedication

We held the dedication services for the current sanctuary in July 2007. Brother Charles Drew from Southport, North Carolina preached the dedication service. Eight of Wilbur and Peggy's children were present for this service. Those attending included: Joyce Cory, June Perry, Shirley Strange, Larry Shemwell, Diann Joines, Deborah Morris, Vickie Avery, and Keith Shemwell. A framed memoir to Elder Shemwell and his wife was presented to the church. The frame was made from wood taken from the original building.

THE SIBLINGS

BRO. DREW AND BRO. SHEMWELL

Tornado!

February 5, 2008, was an exceptionally warm day for winter time in Kentucky. Our midweek service is held on Tuesday night at 7:30. We had assembled this particular night for service as usual. It usually doesn't take long for folks to begin to worship God. On this night, things got wound up fairly quickly. The music was loud; and the saints were worshiping and praising the Lord. Maybe within 30 minutes into the service, the power went out. The saints kept on having church and praising the Lord with the emergency lighting. We were not even aware of what was taking place outside. My first indication of anything out of the ordinary was blue and red lights flashing. This caught someone's attention, and they went to see what had happened outside. Unbeknownst to any of us, an F-3 tornado had traveled 12 miles through our county—through Greenville, Powderly, and Central City-- killing 3 people not far from the church. More than 20 people were injured and over 100 homes were damaged. The width of the tornado averaged 325 yards, with winds reaching 160 mph. At the time, the storm was part of the deadliest tornado outbreak in the United States in more than 20 years. It had actually come within inches of where we were all praising God. It had toppled some landscaping blocks right beside the church and clipped the corner of the overhang. But the Master of the Wind said, "You can't go there!"

The tornado turned at that point and headed across the road and turned in a different direction. Next, it totally destroyed a motel and heavily damaged several homes in the Gas Light Park subdivision in Central City.

It had totally wiped out a used car lot beside us, actually picking up the vehicles and carrying them away. They never rebuilt and we currently own the lot today for parking and a playground. A vehicle traveling from WalMart was picked up in front of the church and flipped, almost directly in front of our church.

We were amazed and shocked as we drove through the county the next day and surveyed the intense damage. All that remained of a steel frame building not far from the church was a pile of twisted rubbish.

I'm so glad "I know the Master of the wind. I know the Maker of the rain. He can calm the storms and make the sun shine again. I know the Master of the winds."

TORNADO DAMAGE

FLIPPED CAR VERY CLOSE TO THE CHURCH. BELOW: BUILDING NEXT TO US (OLD D & P CAR LOT). WE CURRENTLY OWN THIS LOT FOR PARKING AND PLAYGROUND.

18-WHEELER THAT GOT TURNED OVER

RIGHT NEXT DOOR TO US. POWER POLE BROKE AND DESTROYED.

SPEC BUILDING IN GREENVILLE DESTROYED. STEEL FRAME BUILDING ENDED UP AS A PILE OF RUBBISH.

Trusting God—A Forgotten Message

Brother Shemwell had been diagnosed with diabetes in the 1960s and had a lot of trouble with his kidneys. He suffered with kidney stones, having one kidney surgically removed in 1959. During emergency surgery, it burst and urine went all over the ceiling. It was the size of a football.

Not long after, one morning at 3:00, God woke him. He was lying across the bed. God spoke to Him and said, "How can I trust you if you can't trust me?"

Thus, began his journey of trusting God for healing. Although, as far as he knew, he still had diabetes, he told his wife, "Throw away all my medication. Cook for me like you do everyone else. I'm gonna trust God from here on out." He claimed God healed him right then and there of sugar diabetes. I've heard him testify many times, "I can eat all the 'nanner puddin' I want now."

He lived and preached the "Trusting God" message until God called him home.

He suffered a lot with his legs and lower extremities. In 1977, he had many complications. One of his legs swelled really bad from the knee down. It turned all colors. His big toe on that foot rotted off and the toe next to it nearly did, too. He was completely bedfast during the latter part of 1977. He appeared to be on his deathbed, unless God performed a miracle. People from everywhere began to hear about him and come to visit and pray for him. Things looked very bleak. Finally, one day, his leg burst open from the knee down---all the way to the bone! The infection that drained nearly filled up a quart jar. Sister Shemwell pulled white stringy stuff out of it---stuff she literally had to get the scissors and cut off. No salve, medication, or anything was ever placed or rubbed on it. All he asked was for it to be kept clean. God sent an angel that stepped into that room. He fully recovered and lived an additional 8 years. He passed away in January 1986.

His daughter Joyce was backslid at the time of this

happening. She was convinced diabetes was causing his problems. She got one the test strips to check his urine, since he would have to urinate in a container. He was not aware that she did this. When the test came back negative, everyone was convinced he was definitely healed of diabetes.

PEGGY AND WILBUR SHEMWELL

A New Era

Sister Shemwell was never interested in remarrying after Wilbur passed away. Some of the children would tease her from time to time, but she replied, "My only sweetheart is buried in Rose Hill Cemetery."

After many months, life returned to normal following Brother Shemwell's passing. She had children, grandchildren, and a church family that required her attention. Anytime something traumatic happened, she was one of the first ones called. She was a faithful saint of God. She loved her times working in the garden and putting up the produce. She spent time sewing all her clothing. She was truly a Proverbs 31 woman. She never had the fine things in life and never even owned a driver's license, but she was an angel in disguise sent to earth for "such a time as this."

Sister Shemwell suffered many times with gall bladder problems. Although the problem was not officially diagnosed, because she never sought medical attention, she had some rough days and weeks.

During one episode, Ronnie had called the children in, because she wasn't doing well. She lay on the bed unresponsive. Ronnie and his family lived with her after the passing of her husband. He crawled up in the bed with her, prayed for her, and began to speak in her ear. He was trying to get a response of some kind---not willing to say goodbye.

As the children all gathered around, they began singing songs about Jesus. It wasn't long before she opened her eyes and began to sing along. Ronnie asked her, "Mama, do you know who these people are?"

She answered, "Why, sure, I know. These are my children... these are God's children."

God raised her up for many more years.

She was privileged to attend her very first ladies' retreat hosted by the home church on March 13-14, 1998. Sister Ethel Daniel from Jacks Creek, Tennessee, preached for us. Sister Shemwell had read her books and heard about her and always wanted to meet her. When Sister Shemwell walked in, Sister Daniel made the comment, "She's as straight as an arrow."

She meant for her age that she appeared to be in very good health.

The weekend following the ladies' retreat, her daughter Shirley said Sister Shemwell did not act exactly right when she took her home. She seemed to not be able to pick her foot up to exit the car. She appeared to be having mini strokes. Everyone thought she would recover as all times before, but God had other plans.

She was actually incapacitated by that following Tuesday. For one week, we dismissed church services as everyone gathered around her bedside. The house was full around the clock. Church folks and family members gathered around and sang and had church. Since she was not able to attend church, we took church to her. As the seizures began to worsen, everyone did what they could to make her comfortable. She witnessed to everyone that came in until she went unconscious. One of the last things she spoke about was a melody she heard just beyond the river. One of the children asked her how far away it was. She replied, "Three miles."

Three days later, she was taken home to be with Jesus, on March 23, 1998. She deserves to be placed in the 11th chapter of Hebrews among the "Heroes of Faith."

PEGGY

MOTHER OF THE
YEAR AWARD

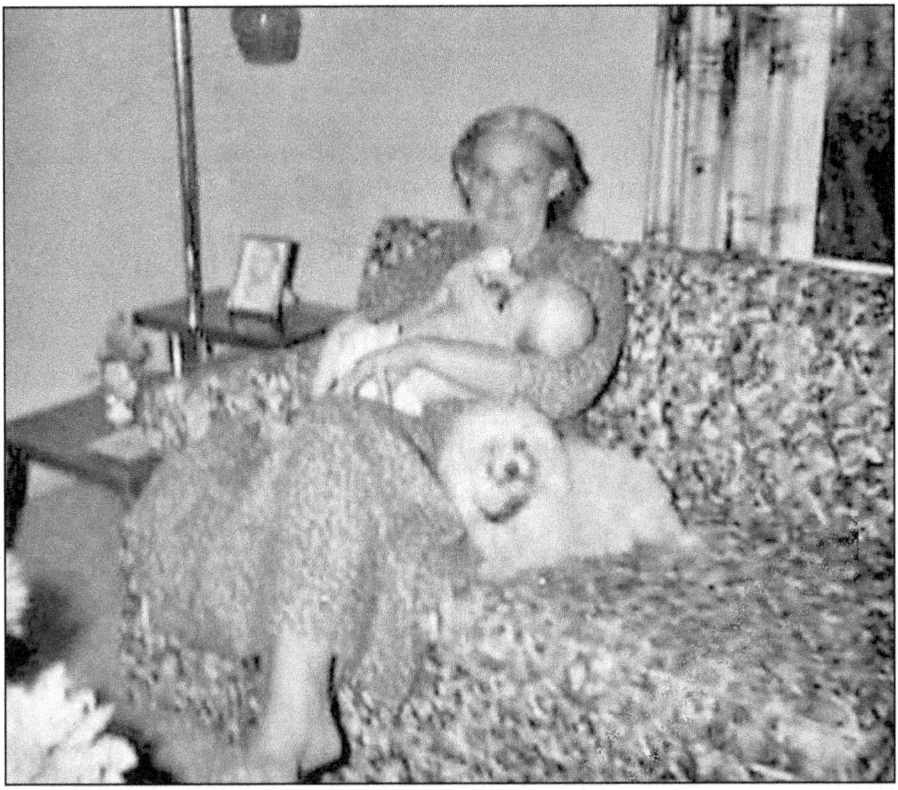

MOTHER
OF THE YEAR AWARD

This is to certify that

Sister Peggy Shemwell

has been named MOTHER OF THE YEAR,
in recognition of her warm understanding, her patient caring,
and her selfless love.
These fine qualities, in addition to her devoted performance of other Motherly Functions,
make her the unanimous choice for the MOTHER OF THE YEAR award, entitling her to
one full day of rest and being waited on and a lifetime of gratitude and love.

Signed with love this 7th day of June, 19 85.
By Powderly Apostolic Holiness Church
and Christian School

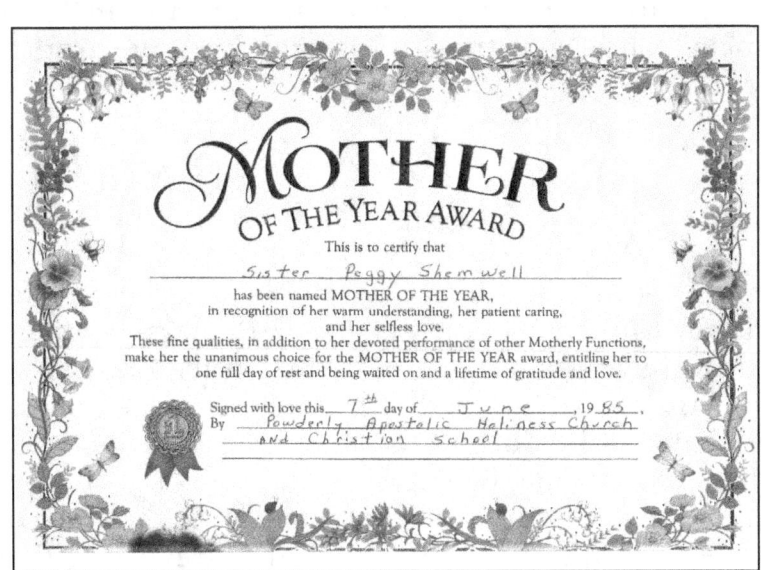

A Baby Boy

Wilbur and Peggy had 5 daughters; then were blessed with their first son—Larry Wilbur on June 15, 1945. When Larry was a baby, he had some issues with his breathing. There were times Peggy would have to shake him to get him to breathe. He would turn blue. Wilbur went and talked to the doctor about the baby, but in the meantime called for prayer. Brother Bud Bivins and Brother Will Johnson came to the house to pray for the baby. There were no flashing lights nor great signs from heaven. They just prayed, ran around the Warm Morning stove, and said the job was done. After they left, Peggy continued having to shake the baby for about 30 minutes. Then something in his throat burst and she grabbed the receiving blanket and began pulling the stuff out of his mouth. Later, Larry got down on the floor and began to play. He never had any more problems with his breathing. Wilbur saw the doctor the next day. The doctor said, "I guess you have come to tell me the baby is dead."

Wilbur said, "No. He's much alive!"

God, in His Divine plan, had a place for Larry in Powderly, Kentucky. The Devil tried to destroy him, but God didn't allow it.

Larry

Another time, when Larry was in 4th grade, he had tumors to appear on his head. He was taken to the doctor to have them burnt off. They stuck out and would bleed if they were bumped or hit. He heard the doctors tell his parents, "If he doesn't have any more by the time he is 16 years old, he may be okay."

Larry had torment from that time until the mid 1960s. Anytime he would get a headache, the Devil was there to assure him that the tumors had come back. One night, he was at a church service at the Crossing Holiness Church. It was a dead service. He had a bad headache and went up for prayer. They anointed him with oil in the Name of the Lord and began to pray. It felt just like a cool breeze entered the front of his head and went all the way through to the back. As the virtue entered in, the headache left. When it went halfway through his head, it was as if he had one-half headache. The torment and pain left. Brother Sherman Arnold was standing behind him and said, "I got that boy's headache."

To this day, he has never had another headache and he is 72 years old.

God was definitely paving the way for the next pastor.

Pastor Larry & Tilda Shemwell Family

God has blessed us with 12 wonderful children: Larry Shemwell, Jr.; Deanna Drake (deceased); Tonya Farber; Steven Kirk Shemwell (deceased); Danika Drake; Jeremy, Brandon, Derek, and Justin Shemwell; Brittany Young; and Ashley Whitehouse. I am thankful to God for allowing me to be able to homebirth my last 6 children. I have witnessed most of my grandchildren's homebirths, as well as a few of my great-grandchildren's homebirths. We also have 48 grandchildren and 15 great-grandchildren.

(Tilda) We got married on March 9, 1963. I was not raised in the holiness faith. Larry's dad was pastor of Powderly Holiness Church. We lived in Hammond, Indiana, for 2 years during the early years of our marriage (1965-67). We attended church at Brother James Holt's when we lived in Hammond. We tried to drive home as often as we could to be in church services at home. The night we repented, we went to church with Beverly and Eugene Uzzle to "Snow Hill" in Hartford, Kentucky. The pastor was Elder Phillip Uzzle. We both repented in November 1966 and were baptized in Jesus' Name in February 1967. It was very cold the day we were baptized---raining, sleeting, and snowing. I had just had Deanna 3 weeks before. When we went to change clothes, my mom told me, "It will kill you." I'm glad to report it killed the old man, but it saved my soul. I received the Holy Ghost in the summer of 1967. Larry received the Holy Ghost sometime later.

LARRY'S FAMILY

The Call

(Larry) When I was feeling my call to preach, I began to question God. I did not take this calling lightly, and I wanted to make sure it was God speaking to me. One of the things I asked God to do was to give me a congregation of nothing but preachers to speak to. Lo and behold, it wasn't long before I received an invitation in the mail from Sister Blankenship. There was going to be a meeting in Madisonville, Kentucky, of nothing but preachers, and I had been invited! No one even knew I was feeling my call at that time. I knew it had to be God! I went and never questioned it again. This was about 1976.

The call into the ministry has a lot of ups and downs and ins and outs. I was not seeking the position to pastor. The responsibility to pastor was placed upon my shoulders when my dad was no longer able to fill that position in

1977. I worked a full-time job as well as pastored during the first 9 years. When I realized this was not working out and I needed to quit my job and devote my time completely to the church, I consulted my supervisor. I was working at the Caney Creek coal mine at the time making good money. I could not count on the church to provide the same level of income that I was making at the coal mine. The supervisor was not happy about my decision and did not want me to leave. He told me to just take a 3-month leave of absence and reconsider. This had never been offered before in the history of that mines. I took the 3 months and went back to inform him that I could not stay. I can say that God has never let us down. It has never been about the money. It's fulfilling the calling God has placed on my life. Our church is a very free-hearted group of people. They have provided for my family and many others in need.

Prior to building our current sanctuary, we had been debt free for several years. We paid for everything we could before borrowing any money. We ended up having to borrow a $100,000 note to finish the building. When we made the first payment of $1100, I realized $900+ was going toward interest. We feverishly began working to pay the note off and became debt free within 18 months.

Since that time, God allowed us to be able to buy the two adjacent properties to us and pay cash for them.

Our Miracles

God has worked in many miraculous ways in our home. We trusted God for healing when 2 of our children had broken arms. Danika fell on her arm and broke it near the wrist. Brandon fell out of a tall tree and broke his arm in 2 places. He almost went into shock. The social services were called to investigate Brandon's broken arm. They came to our home and said, "You did a good job taking care of it." We never heard another thing from them and God took care of both of the children with no after effects.

(Tilda) On January 20, 1987, my last child Ashley was born at home. The delivery went fine, but I started hemorrhaging immediately following delivery. I was going in and out of consciousness as I began to lose a lot of blood. Larry was by my side through it all. He could see me begin to lose my color. I was yawning a lot and the inside of my mouth looked chalky. My oldest daughter had left with the other children to go to church right before she was born. Someone contacted the church for prayer. We lived in a two-story house. I was in an upstairs bedroom. The lower level began to fill up with church folks as they intreated God in prayer. I began to think, "Deanna is going to have to raise my children." I almost told Larry to keep the children together. I don't know who touched God, but He definitely stepped into that room. He stopped the hemorrhaging and added 30 more years to my life. God gave me a wonderful experience through this. I'm so thankful He allowed me to raise my children, to work in the Christian school for 20 years, to be able to see my children graduate, to see them get married, and to be able to enjoy my grandchildren.

Donald & Vickie Avery Family

We have been blessed with 3 children: Vickie Karen Zguro, Donald Shane Avery, and David Franklin Avery.

We also have 12 grandchildren: Tyler Shane Avery, Johnna Rae Zguro, Katera Nicole Avery, Faith Ann Avery, Vickie Kaitlyn Zguro, Braxton Avery, Brayden Avery, Kason Avery, Parker Avery, Lacy Avery, Summer Zguro, and Kenneth B. Zguro.

(Donald) I first came to the church in 1967 when it started. I helped mop floors and clean the church. I repented in 1966 and received the Holy Ghost in 1977.

Vickie's dad was the first pastor of the church. She was taken to church all her life. But she repented in 1977 and received the Holy Ghost in February 1995.

(Vickie) In June 1989, we were on our way to Nashville, Tennessee. We had just come through Central City on Highway 431 south. As we neared a railroad crossing, the lights weren't working. We never realized a train was coming, until we started to cross the tracks. I tried to turn the car to go down the gravel roadbed. I did not have the Holy Ghost at the time. I remember thinking, "Oh God, have mercy!"

I never remember the impact. It was like I passed out prior to that. The train actually hit the car and pushed it to the side. It was only a miracle that we were not all killed. When I came to, the paramedics had gotten me out of the car and laid me on the highway. I remember telling them to get my pastor---Larry Shemwell. I had hit my head on the windshield. My face looked scary from all the swelling and bruises.

When my brother Larry arrived, I remember him shaking me and telling me to hold on.

They ended up transporting us to the hospital. Of course, the car was totaled. I had bruising and a broken arm. Donnie had chest contusions. Karen almost bit her lip completely off. They had to do surgery on it. One of the boys had a cut on his knee. The other boy and Billy Zguro had no injuries.

No one can ever tell me there isn't a God and He doesn't dispatch guardian angels in situations like this! I know beyond the shadow of a doubt that God was there on Highway 431 that day!

DONNIE AND VICKIE AVERY

Willie & Darlene Bates Family

(Darlene) I repented, was baptized in Jesus' Name, and received the Holy Ghost in 1975.

Willie and I met at Brenda and Tony Mills's wedding in Hickman, Kentucky, in December 1980. Willie attended the Church of Jesus Christ pastored by Elder James Uzzle. Willie said when I walked in the room at the reception and he saw me, it was "love at first sight." I didn't exactly know how I felt about that. In January 1981, we began our courtship. Willie neither owned a driver's license nor vehicle. Elder Uzzle or one of the church members would bring Willie to Central City to court me. Willie would stay with Paul and Frances Uzzle; I would go visit my Aunt Vickie. She lived across the road from them. We were married on May 9, 1981.

Editor's Note: It was absolutely a match made in heaven!

We lived in Hickman, Kentucky, for a few years after we married. I was so lonesome and homesick. Willie agreed to move me back to Muhlenberg County. We had a new house built in Moorman, Kentucky. Willie ended up getting his driver's license, and we got a car. We arose on a morning in December 1988, and I wanted to go to WalMart. We lived about 10 miles away. Willie hardly denied me anything I wanted. I was his "baby." But some reason, that morning he said we shouldn't go. I begged and pleaded until Willie gave in. During this time, I had quit reading my Bible and praying. I had not backslid. My mom and Willie tried to encourage me to be more dedicated. We got to the post office in South Carrollton. A car decided to pass and hit us head-on. I went into shock. When they loaded me in the ambulance, I was hollering, "Jesus!"

We were bruised up, the wreck messed up my spleen, and I was placed in ICU.

By God's mercies, we both recovered; but it was definitely a wake-up call for me.

On September 29, 2002, we were in church on a Sunday

morning. I never liked going to Sunday morning services; but thank God, we were there that morning! As the worship service was in full swing, Willie died on the front pew! Sister Danika was singing the song "One Way Flight to Gloryland." Willie began experiencing some difficulties unknown to everyone around us and sat down on the front pew. He grabbed his chest, his head fell back on the pew, he slumped down in the pew, his eyes rolled back in his head, and he DIED!! His color had turned an ashen gray. Immediately everyone noticed. I fell apart! The church folks began to gather around and cry out to God. They began to holler, "Jesus," in one accord. Someone felt for a pulse. There was none. As everyone continued calling on God, Willie awoke, opened his eyes, and looked around.

It was a NOTABLE miracle. Once again, God had walked into the room. He knew I wasn't prepared for losing Willie at that time. We both walked out of the church together at dismissal and went home.

When Willie's time came to go, it happened again on a Sunday morning. We were home taking care of my Mom. She was bedfast and lived with us. Willie heard sirens; a building was on fire a few doors down. He walked to the back room. I heard a noise, went to check, and found him lying in the floor dead. I was never going to be prepared for this day, but I DO thank God for extending his life so many times.

WILLIE AND DARLENE BATES'S WEDDING
(SHOWN WITH ELDER & SISTER SHEMWELL)

45

Daniel & Kendra Bennett Family

God has been so good to us. He blessed us with two sons and two daughters: Jake, Kylar, Kenleigh, and Emree.

(Daniel) I repented and was baptized in Jesus' Name in October 2007. I was attending the Crossing Holiness Church. Josiah Whitehouse invited me to Powderly Holiness Church. I made it my home church about 6 months later.

When I first came to God, I didn't know much about trusting God for the healing of my body. I had been taking antibiotics for an abscessed tooth. I wanted to be right. I told God that I would quit taking them. I fleeced God by telling Him that if the abscess returned, I would start taking the antibiotics again. If it didn't return, I would continue to trust Him. I ended up throwing those pills away about a month later.

(Kendra) I was born and raised in the church. I repented, was baptized in Jesus' Name, and received the Holy Ghost in March 2009.

I gave birth to all my children in homebirths. I was attended by midwives in the church.

DANIEL & KENDRA BENNETT

DaKota & Allison Brooks Family

God has blessed us with three very special children: Easton, Quaiden, and Paris AliAnna.

(Allison) I was born and raised in the church. I repented, was baptized in Jesus' Name, and received the Holy Ghost in August 2012.

God blessed us with our 3 children during homebirths. I was attended by midwives in our church.

(DaKota) God allowed me to meet Allison and opened my eyes to the truth. I received the Holy Ghost during the homebirth of our first son on May 27, 2013.

ALLISON AND CODY'S FAMILY

Brandon & Erica Byrne Family

God blessed us with two healthy children: our son, Peyton and our daughter, Shaelyn.

(Erica) I was born and raised in the church. I repented and was baptized in Jesus' Name the latter part of 2012 and received the Holy Ghost in January 2013.

I gave birth to both of my children in homebirths.

Brandon had tried other churches but was searching for truth when he first came to the church.

ERICA, BRANDON, AND CHILDREN

Mike & Ruthie Camacho Family

God blessed us with one special and beautiful daughter: Keirra Camacho.

(Ruthie) We first came to the church in April 2010. I always knew there was more to God's plan. I was also under heavy conviction. I repented in May 2010, was baptized in Jesus' Name in July 2010, and received the Holy Ghost in August 2011.

God brought me from a world of drugs and alcohol. Jesus also healed Keirra from a 106 degree temperature for about 2 weeks. Mike has been delivered from high blood pressure and diabetes, no longer having to take his medication. Most of all Jesus opened our eyes to Truth!

FAMILY PICTURE OF MIKE AND RUTHIE

Bethany Daniel

I was born and raised in the church. My parents attended and took me to church all my life.

I repented October 26, 2014; I was baptized November 23, 2014; and received the Holy Ghost in November 2014.

I don't have a testimony like most people. I have never tried drugs, alcohol, cigarettes, or anything like that. But I'm thankful that God kept me from those things. I'm also thankful that I was raised in a Christian home. I'm thankful that I know truth and have a good church.

BETHANY DANIEL

Greg & Amy Daniel Family

We have been blessed with 10 children: Greg, Jr.; Micah; Blaine; Shea; Cailin; Ashley; Kylie; Isaac; Emilee; and Ava. God delivered them all in homebirths.

(Amy) Greg was born and raised in the church. His parents had attended and taken him to church his entire life. He repented when he was 9 years old and received the Holy Ghost when he was 13 years old.

I started attending Powderly Holiness Church in 1989 when I was 11 years old. My parents enrolled my siblings in the Powderly Christian School. We were formerly in the trinity doctrine, but Daddy saw the truth on one God and Jesus' Name baptism. He was so excited about it and wanted everyone to know. But just because Daddy saw the revelation of Jesus' Name didn't mean that I saw it. Everyone in my family was enlightened, except me. I tried so hard to understand it, but it just didn't make sense to me. This went on for several years. I wanted to feel it and see what Daddy was feeling, but I couldn't. I would pray, and I even got baptized in Jesus' Name, without having the full understanding. I repented and was baptized in 1996. I remember praying, "God, who are You? I feel You, but I don't understand who You really are."

Sometime later, we came back to the sanctuary from our Sunday School classes. As I was walking through the church doors, Sister Sharon Shemwell was teaching on one God. She read I Timothy 3:16: "And without controversy, great is the mystery of godliness: God was manifest in the flesh, justified in the Spirit, seen of angels, preached unto the Gentiles, believed on in the world, received up into glory."

When I heard that verse, immediately my understanding was opened and I saw it. I was so excited I could have run around the church! It made sense how the Father, Son, and Holy Ghost were ONE. Now He wasn't just Daddy's God; He became mine also.

We have witnessed God perform many miracles in our home and for our family. I would like to share a few with you.

When I was 9 years old, I was riding my bike and had a wreck and landed on the handle bar. It punctured my stomach. We never realized at the time how serious the injury was. I began getting very sick, was not able to keep my food down, and was in a lot of pain. My body was beginning to lock up on me. I was attending a public school in Ohio County. The school nurse sent a paper home explaining to my parents that I could not come back to school, until I was checked out by a doctor. We didn't know anything about trusting God. Mom took me to see the doctor and he took x-rays. I was so scared when the doctor came back with the results. He said the handlebar from my bike had punctured my intestines and my guts were hanging out of them. I had developed gangrene wrapped around my intestines. That was the cause of the green vomit and the foul smell. I was basically dying. He explained that if I threw up one more time, I would require emergency surgery. Mama said she needed to talk to my Dad.

We went home and talked. I was scared; I didn't want surgery. We were in revival at that time. (Remember, we didn't know anything about trusting God.) I told my parents that I did not want surgery—to just pray. They were so worried, but they also wanted to pray. They had a prayer line that night at church. Daddy wanted me to get prayer. I told Daddy to get in the line for me and Jesus would heal me. Daddy stood in my place and had prayer; I watched as the glory came down. Immediately, I was healed. I'm still fine today—with NO surgery. Praise God!

My husband is a drywall contractor. He was at work, fell down some steps, and hit his back on the corner of the steps. He was in extreme pain for 3 days. He was in bed and couldn't move for 2 weeks. We did not know what the outcome would be. He was told that he had possibly broken his back. He totally trusted God for the healing of his body.

God is faithful! He totally recovered. He has no back pain to this day and is able to perform anything that needs to be done.

When our seventh child Kylie was born, her umbilical cord was rotting. It had holes in it and was turning black. We thought she was dead when she was first born. But prayer was made and God allowed us to keep her.

My oldest son Greg broke both his arms when he fell out of a treehouse. The breaks were very bad. We trusted God and He moved! His arms are straight and normal today.

My son Blaine also broke his arm. God healed him also, and his arm is straight and normal today.

Our fourth child Amy Shea had a bad skin disorder. It occurred at six months of age and continued until she was two years old. She looked like she was burnt all over. She cried all the time. I did everything I knew to do, but it only got worse. One night at church, deliverance came. God moved! The next day, we saw immediate changes. Today she is completely healed.

GREG AND AMIE

GREG'S CHILDREN

Joseph Daniel

I was born and raised in the church. My parents had taken me to church all my life.

I repented on November 1, 2015, and was baptized 2 days later.

JOSEPH DANIEL

Timothy & Hannah Daniel Family

God has blessed us with 2 very precious sons: Samuel and Titus. God blessed me with a home delivery with both of my babies with no complications.

I repented and was baptized at 7 years old; I received the Holy Ghost when I was 14 years old.

TIMOTHY AND HANNAH DANIEL FAMILY

Mama

My Mother Deanna Drake left us on December 22, 2015. I would like to share her beautiful testimony about trusting God. Deliverance does not always come in the form of healing.

"Now faith is the substance of things hoped for, the evidence of things not seen. For by it the elders obtained a good report." (Hebrews 11:1-2)

Mama started having some difficulties in the summer of 2013. She had hemorrhaged after I was born for 12+ years. She never was able to have anymore children. I was her miracle baby. She had a knot to come up. She felt like she may have had fibroid tumors. She started taking an all-natural supplement that was supposed to dissolve them. One day, she felt like God spoke to her and said, "I don't need any help." She quit taking it for awhile and tried to start it again later. Again she felt like she shouldn't do it. She went and threw it in the dumpster.

She was not one to complain and was always concerned about her ten siblings; therefore no one was aware for awhile of what was going on. She went on a gluten-free diet thinking this would help her situation. She did drop some weight and looked very nice. Everyone just thought her weight loss was due to her change of diet. But as the weight began to rapidly fall off, it became noticeable that something just wasn't right. It was Mama's desire to trust the Lord, whatever the outcome. She made this very clear to me, my Dad, and everyone else. She didn't want to hear anyone talking negative.

As time went on, her abdomen begin to increase in size from the affliction. It actually looked like she was expecting. She hid things for awhile by wearing loose flowing clothing. But it was finally difficult for her to find anything to wear. The pain was so great. It hurt my heart so bad to see her this way. Samuel was born about a month before she became this way. He loved to visit Nana;

he loved to crawl up in the bed with her and play trucks on the mattress.

She attended church as long as she was able. She loved camping and wanted to keep things as normal as possible for my Dad. So she agreed to go on one more camping trip with him in October 2015. The trip to the Smoky Mountains was almost unbearable for her. She had to lie down in the truck most of the way there. Even after arriving, there was very little she could do. But her family was her priority, coming in second after her God.

She would lie in her bed during her last few months and call or text everyone in the church that was discouraged or having a difficult time and try to lift them up. She contacted some of these people on a daily basis.

During her last few weeks, the pain grew very intense. She was not able to eat and was getting very little rest. The growth was also affecting her ability to breathe freely. It had grown extremely large. Many well-meaning individuals tried to diagnose her and urged her to get help. Yet her reply was always the same, "If God doesn't do it, it just won't get done. There is no alternative."

Flesh sometimes looks at circumstances like these and thinks that we have lost the battle. Yet God's ways are not our ways. We were not put on this earth to live forever.

"These all died in faith, not having received the promises, but having seen them afar off, and were persuaded of them, and embraced them, and confessed that they were strangers and pilgrims on the earth.

For they that say such things declare plainly that they seek a country.

And truly, if they had been mindful of that country from whence they came out, they might have had opportunity to have returned.

But now they desire a better country, that is, an heavenly: wherefore God is not ashamed to be called their God: for he hath prepared for them a city." (Hebrews 11:13-16)

On Sunday, two days before she passed, I broke down

on her bed, very emotional, and told her, "This is not okay." I knew unless God performed a miracle, she was leaving us.

I said, "Mama, this can't happen." I did not want to lose my Mama. She was my best friend—my everything in the whole world!

She said, "You don't need to look at the present, but the future."

I didn't understand at the time what she was talking about. The future? There looked like no future for us. I have since come to grips that she was talking about our eternal future.

She worried about the baby I was expecting. I had been staying up with her countless nights. I was struggling to stay awake at times. I had stayed on Sunday night and left on Monday morning to get some rest. But when I went home, I could not rest; because I knew my Mama was not doing well at all. The ones staying with her contacted me and asked me to bring her some Sonic ice. I stopped by Sonic to get her some ice. I stayed to do what I could that day. Jordan had been staying and helping her. They insisted that I go home that night and get some rest. I did not want to leave. Mama reached over and patted my stomach and said, "That's my grandbaby in there. You must take care of him."

She insisted that I go home that night and get some rest. She said, "I will be okay."

I said, "Will you promise me, Mama, that you will be okay?"

She said, "Yes."

That same night, the ladies from the church gathered in the house to pray and to sing with her. She was in so much pain and could not even lie down, because her breathing was getting so labored. The pain in her back was VERY intense. We all went home, trying to believe God for a miracle. She received her angel's wings early the next morning. Is this not what living for God is all about? Preparing to live with Him forever? Or is it to build our own little kingdom here on earth?

I can honestly say the things of this earth lost their value to her. She was no longer interested in them, but rather was interested in going to her new home and taking everyone with her that she could. I'm so thankful she held fast her integrity.

"I Want Us to Be Together in Heaven"

I
You may have a fancy car,
A brand new house that shines by far
You may live to be a hundred years old.
But if you have not been saved,
It all ends with the grave.
But I want us to be together in heaven.

II
You may be a millionaire
Wearing clothes beyond compare
You may have the best that money can buy
But if the blood is not applied
Then in hell you'll lift your eyes
But I want us to be together in heaven.

Chorus
I want us to be together in heaven
I want to walk down the street of pure gold
I want to run through the field of green clover
See the mansion, smell the flowers
Hear them singing it's all ours
See the rivers gently flowing
Feel the gentle breezes blowing
I want us to be together in heaven.

DEANNA DRAKE

Editor's Note: When Deanna Drake first became expecting with Hannah, she attended a Bible study my husband and I were sharing with the young people from the church. This was the latter part of January 1992. The topic that night was "The Praises of God Are a Stop Sign to the Devil." We talked about the different forms of praise and the importance of praising the Lord in every circumstance we encounter. Right when the Bible study was wrapping up, Sister Deanna went to the restroom. She called for her friend to come and help her. They called for me, since I was a midwife. It was a scary sight when I opened the door. It looked as if an animal had been slaughtered in there. We immediately asked for prayer. Then I recalled what we had been studying about, and realized it was time to put it into action. I told Sister Deanna, "Start praising the Lord. The praises of God are a stop sign to the Devil."

She had no intention of seeking medical attention, because she planned on trusting God for this pregnancy and delivery. We cleaned everything up, and she was taken home. It would have definitely appeared that she had lost the baby. Time went on and she thought she had again conceived, but was unsure of the due date. Miraculously, Hannah Carie Drake was born on August 25, 1992—about 7 months following this episode. She was a full-term baby, so there's no doubt in my mind that God walked into the room and preserved life that day when the Devil tried to take it. Deanna was not able to have any additional children. Her mission was accomplished on this earth in December 2015. She absolutely adored Hannah and her little grandson Samuel. Titus arrived after her decease.

Tony & Deborah Daniel Family

We have been blessed with a wonderful family. God blessed us with thirteen children: Tony Daniel, Jr.; Teleah Rust; Greg Daniel; Jennifer Waddell; Kristi Whitehouse; Deborah Shuttleworth; Stephanie Dean; Steven Daniel; Timothy Daniel; Allison Brooks; Bethany, Joseph, and Kyle Daniel.

We also have 27 grandchildren.

(Deborah) I first came as a visitor when my Uncle Larry and Aunt Tilda Shemwell invited us. I repented and was baptized in Jesus' Name in September 1975. I received the Holy Ghost in December 1985.

Tony repented and was baptized in September 1975. He received the Holy Ghost in December 1975.

The Lord has blessed both of us very much through our 42-year journey of living for God. When we first married in 1977, money was very tight and work was scarce. Jesus always provided everything we needed and paid many bills when there was no money. He has brought groceries to our doorstep when there were no groceries in the house. He blessed us with thirteen wonderful children, while we trusted God in homebirths. When the children got sick, the only thing we knew to do was to ask for prayer and to trust in God. He has always moved for us; maybe not when we wanted, but just in time.

After my fifth delivery with Kristi, my placenta did not pass. While trying to get it to deliver, the cord broke off completely. The placenta remained inside of me. We did not seek medical attention, choosing rather to trust God to take care of the situation. We knew the risks involved, but also knew we served a God that was able to do anything. A woman had just died in Tennessee with the same complications. Twenty-four hours later, the placenta delivered with no complications and no side effects.

When my first daughter Teleah was a baby, I noticed

one morning that her upper leg had turned black for no reason. Prayer was made and the discoloration soon disappeared.

When Greg was about one year old, he got very sick with what appeared to be pneumonia. Jesus came on the scene and delivered once again.

Jesus has done nothing but good for our family, and we are forever grateful.

TONY AND DEBBIE DANIEL FAMILY

Billy & Carolyn Deaton Family

We have three children: Samantha Spence, Kristin Alonzo, and Andrea Anderson.

We also have 10 grandchildren.

I was raised Catholic and had never even opened a Bible until I was 21 years old. I was living in California in 1984 and happened to be going through a divorce. My dad Jerry Peck was attending Powderly Holiness Church at the time. He invited me and my daughter Kristin to come to Kentucky to live. Two weeks after I arrived, I repented. I was baptized in Jesus' Name two weeks following my conversion.

When Kristin was about a year old, I had my first trial. I was a new convert and had never been taught to trust God for healing. This was two weeks after I repented. She got very sick with a high fever. Taking her to a doctor never entered my mind. I gave her to God and said, "Take her or leave her with me." He chose to leave her with me.

My grandson Tanner and I were in an intersection. We were in a very small car. A truck ran a red light and shaved off my front bumper. Praise God for His guardian angels! We were not even hurt.

My daughter Kristin was expecting her second child Olivia. The doctors could see on the ultrasound things were not developing properly and tried three times to talk her into terminating the pregnancy (abortion). She vehemently told them, "No!"

Five months later, Olivia Grace Caroline Fuentes was born with hydrocephalus (water on the brain). Kristin had been told the baby would have all sorts of abnormalities. She had none, except the hydrocephalus. Olivia is currently in sixth grade and getting very good grades. She has never had any handicaps.

In 2009, my husband and I owed $72,000 to the IRS. Elder Donald Lance preached a message about decreeing things before the Lord. I decided to put God to His Word and ask largely. Brother Lance, Sister Lovins, and I agreed together in Jesus' Name concerning the debt. Six months later, it was reduced to $15,000!!

Probably the most amazing thing I have witnessed happened in 1988. I received an envelope in the mail with only two $20 bills inside. About 24 hours later, I had to replace the battery in my car. I was a single mom. God provided the need before I even realized I had one. The $40 bought the battery with $1.25 to spare! Thank God for being an on-time God!!

BILLY AND CAROLYN DEATON

BEN AND ANDREA ANDERSON

KRISTIN AND HER FAMILY

JERRY AND CLARA PECK
MY DAD AND CLARA

Katie Drake

I had been taken to church all my life. I started attending Powderly Holiness Church in 2003 when my parents decided to make that our home church.

I repented in 2005, was baptized in Jesus' Name in February 2006, and received the Holy Ghost on August 25, 2010.

Although I was born and raised in the church, I never had my own personal experience. Jesus was just the God my parents talked about. I could not call Him "my" God. After I married in 2012, I faced things I never dreamed I would face—some very hard things. I remember my dad saying to me, "This is your situation. You will have to touch God for yourself."

I now can say that Jesus is the best friend I've ever had. He has been my strength through it all. When I felt I couldn't take another step, He carried me. He kept me through many lonely nights, and He is the best Comforter there is! I'm so glad I can now call Him "my" God!

KATIE DRAKE

Keith & Danika Drake Family

We have been wonderfully blessed with ten sons and one daughter: David, Taylor, Brett, Blake, Jacob, Eric, Kaylee, Kobe, Hayden, Brantly, and Lucas. We are expecting our first grandchild in October 2017.

(Danika) I was born and raised in the church. My Daddypa was my pastor when I repented. Then my dad became pastor in 1977. I repented and was baptized as a child. I received the Holy Ghost on September 28, 1986.

Keith attended Belton Pentecostal Church. We attended his home church the first 2 years of our marriage. Then we started attending Powderly Holiness Church.

I gave birth to all eleven of my children through homebirths. I was attended by midwives in our church.

My son Eric was involved in a bad accident when he was 5 years old. He was run over by a 3000 pound Kabota. He should have died, but God spared Him. His foot was busted open. It was a nasty looking injury. Two weeks later, I pulled grass out of it. God prevented him from developing any kind of infection.

I had something wrong with my body. I developed a knot in the left side of my abdomen. I was in severe pain. I could not even drink without pain. I lost about 14 pounds in 2 weeks. God healed me! The knot is gone and I am fine. We were blessed with our first grandchild on October 19, 2017.

Floyd and Tonya Farber Family

(Tonya) God has blessed me with 3 wonderful children: LaShonda Shaw, Krista Wilken, and Johnathon Render. I have also been blessed with 6 beautiful grandchildren: Kamdin and Terrance Groves; Zaxton and Grayson Shaw; and Klayton and Kourtney Wilken.

I repented and was baptized in Jesus' Name in 1997. I received the Holy Ghost in 2002.

FLOYD AND TONYA FARBER

LASHONDA'S FAMILY

KRISTA AND CHILDREN

TONYA & JOHNATHON

Steven & Rita Findley Family

God blessed us with a wonderful family of 4 girls and 1 boy. Our children are Stephanie Morris, Misty Morris, Amie Daniel, Caleb Findley, and Brittney Horn. We were also blessed with 21 grandchildren.

(Rita) Steven and I both repented in the Church of God. Steven repented in November 1976 and I repented in the beginning of 1977. I received the Holy Ghost not long after I repented; Steven received it in April 1977.

We were both very sincere and excited about living for the Lord. Steven had been talking to different co-workers about the Lord. One of his co-workers attended a Jesus' Name church. Brother Jerry Bratcher, his pastor, from the Hartford Apostolic Church had invited Steven to come to their all-night prayer meeting. Steven was eager to go. Several ministers from various Jesus' Name churches also attended. Brother Bratcher had to leave for a little while. When he returned, he found Steven surrounded by the others. They were telling him he was not in the right doctrine. He needed to believe in one God and be baptized in Jesus' Name and receive the Holy Ghost. Steven said the Lord kept telling him, "Don't deny me."

He said, "What you're saying may be true, but I cannot deny that I've been filled with the Holy Ghost."

You could hear a pin drop.

Brother Bratcher spoke up and said, "Come to my house and we will go through the Scriptures."

At 3:00 A.M., they talked and went through the Scriptures. They read John 20:24-29 about Thomas doubting. When Thomas said, "My Lord and my God," in verse 28, Steven said it was like scales fell from his eyes. He saw the truth. He had been a minister in the Church of God. Later he tried to go back and find trinity verses, but he could not find them. God truly opened his eyes to the truth of Jesus' Name that day! This was the latter part of

1986. We were baptized at the Crossing Holiness Church in January 1987 in the precious Name of Jesus!

Steven was the only member in his family that had been baptized in Jesus' Name.

We started attending the Powderly Holiness Church in October 1989.

I would like to share a special testimony concerning Brother Findley.

October 3, 2005

Steven had gone to Brother Larry's and was taking a starter off from a vehicle. He slipped and hit his stomach hard on the vehicle. He was in so much pain and could hardly drive home. He arrived home and was so sick; he could not even help himself. The sickness progressively grew worse. He was vomiting regularly and losing a lot of weight. Touching his back or smelling different things would make him very sick. He began having spasms in his body. On October 8, his brothers called and said they were coming to check on him. I called Brother Larry and ask him to have the church people to pray. Brother Ryan stopped by on his way to church and said the church would be praying at 7:45. Steven's vision was leaving, but he would struggle to watch the clock. The church family began filling the house. His feet began turning blue; then he grabbed his stomach and fell back. We could not find a pulse. The church began earnestly praying. Megan Whitehouse had arrived with her dad and was sitting in the van waiting on him. She said she felt a powerful force come through and the trailer appeared to be shaking. The power of God was manifested that day. He lurched forward and started grinning. The church family began singing his favorite song. The first stanza goes, "I will draw my strength from Jesus as I lay upon His breast. I will take my comfort from Him. I will find in Him my rest." Steven joined right in. His brothers arrived during this miraculous move of God and tried to convince him to go to the hospital. But he replied, "Don't worry about me.

Jesus has raised me up." After everyone left, he asked for something to eat. Everything went back to normal. Praise God! Jesus let us keep him for 3 more years. Then he went home to Glory still trusting God.

RITA AND STEVE FINDLEY

BELOW: STEVEN FINDLEY

RITA AND CHILDREN

Cathy Gregory

We had lived in Indiana most of my life and would come to Kentucky to visit. My mom's sister is Sister Tilda Shemwell. When we moved to Kentucky in 1974, Sister Tilda invited my mom to church. We started visiting the church. Mom repented in June 1975. At that time, we all started attending church regularly. I repented and was baptized in September 1975. I received the Holy Ghost on March 25, 1977.

I don't have a testimony of all the things God delivered me from in a worldly lifestyle; but God has kept me from cigarettes, drugs, and alcohol. In the 1980's, I was tormented with fear. I was scared all of the time. I didn't want to be left in a room alone. A preacher came to the church and called me out. He told me that I had a fear in me. Then he prayed for me and God delivered me from that fear. Praise the Lord!

CATHY GREGORY

Donald & Barbara Gregory Family

We were blessed with 6 daughters and one son: Deborah Daniel, Diann Brett, Lisa Grogan, Cathy Gregory, Amanda Walker, Michelle Gregory, and Donald Gregory, Jr. (deceased).

We have 26 grandchildren: Tony Lee Daniel, Teleah Rust, Greg Daniel, Jennifer Waddell, Kristi Whitehouse, Deborah Shuttleworth, Stephanie Dean, Steven Daniel, Timothy Daniel, Allison Brooks, Bethany Daniel, Joe Daniel, Kyle Daniel, Darah Risinger, Bryan Grogan, Renae Cataldo, Eric Grogan, Scott Grogan, Austin Grogan, Andrew Grogan, Gregory Brett, Tyler Brett, Tristan Walker, Trace Walker, Dawson Walker, and Rhett Walker, and 32 great-grandchildren.

(Barbara) We started attending Powderly Holiness Church in 1974. We had moved from Indiana to Kentucky. My sister Tilda had invited me. I repented and was baptized in 1975. I received the Holy Ghost in 1992.

Donald repented in 1988.

God has kept me from the things of the world and healed our bodies so many times. He still takes care of us.

DON AND BARBARA GREGORY

LEFT: DON AND BARBARA GREGORY AND CHILDREN

Michelle Gregory

I have been taken to church my entire life. I repented in 2002.

I praise God for life, health, and strength. I love God more than anything and I thank Him for my home and food.

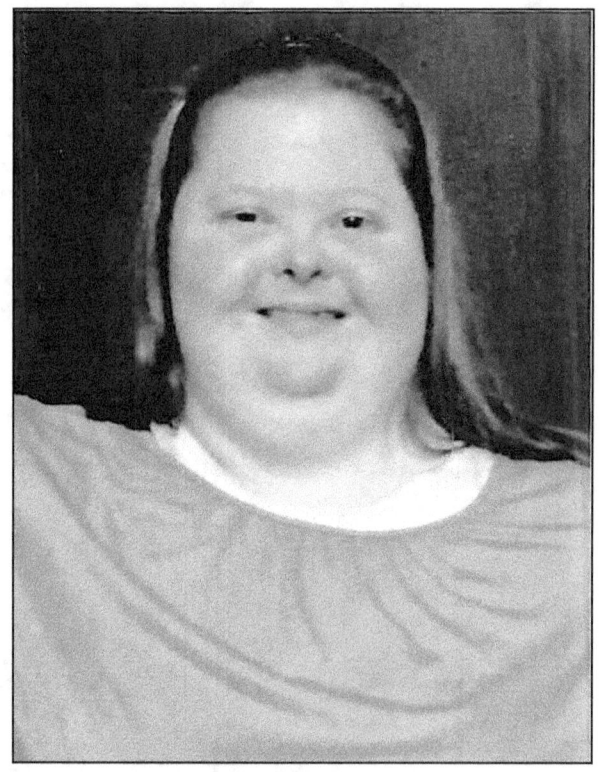

MICHELLE GREGORY

Charles & Gayle Grogan Family

(Gayle) I was taken to church as a child. My dad was the first pastor—Elder Wilbur Shemwell.

I repented in November 1964. I was baptized in Jesus' Name in 1965 and received the Holy Ghost in July 1992.

We are the parents of eight children: Darren Grogan, Gina Morris, Vanessa VanMeter, Barry Grogan, Jared Grogan, Anthony Grogan, Wesley Grogan, and Laura Knight. We have 28 grandchildren and 13 great-grandchildren.

One miracle I saw happen before my very eyes was when God delivered my son Wesley from drugs and alcohol. He was living a very reckless lifestyle. I prayed constantly that God would turn him around. The habits had destroyed his marriage. He had two young sons. God protected him through some accidents that should have been fatal. Finally, he ended up spending time in prison. That was when God really got his attention. We don't always like the roads we have to travel, but God definitely knows what He is doing. He began reading his Bible while incarcerated and attending chapel services. He came out of prison a changed man. God restored his family and he is now living for God. Don't ever give up on those impossible situations. If God did it for me, He can do it for you!

CHARLES AND GAYLE GROGAN FAMILY

Jared & Pamela Grogan Family

God has blessed us with three beautiful daughters: Jarah Ann, Alyssa Jade, and Briley Shaye.

(Pam) I started coming to the church in 1997 with my neighbor Sharon Ball. I repented at a tent meeting in 1997 and was baptized soon after. I received the Holy Ghost on December 27, 1997. Jared was born and raised in the church. He received the Holy Ghost when he was nine years old.

God delivered me from drugs and brought me to the Truth. When Jarah was six years old, she developed a very high fever. Her temperature was 107 degrees. She began having seizures, but the Lord touched her. She came out fine. She hasn't had much fever since. When Alyssa was about 8 months old, she fell from about 10-14 steps on a hard floor. She came through with no injuries. God has been very good to us and moved for us so many times.

JARED AND PAM GROGAN FAMILY

Troy & Nandria Hampton Family

God blessed us with a beautiful daughter Gelane Hope and a handsome son Andrew Durall.

(Nandria) I was raised in the church. I repented, was baptized in Jesus' Name, and received the Holy Ghost all within a four-month period from July-November 2006.

I, myself, am a miracle. At the time I was born, weighing in at 9 pounds, whooping cough was running rampant. A child coughed in my face when I was newborn and not long after, I developed the whooping cough. I would cough so bad that my mom would have to turn me upside down and shake me to get me to breathe. I turned blue many times. Prayer was made and God spared my life.

God also delivered me with my children in homebirths. I was attended by midwives from my church. I have witnessed numerous miracles in my lifetime.

TROY AND NANDRIA HAMPTON FAMILY

Joshua & April Hardin Family

(Joshua) April repented, was baptized in Jesus' Name, and received the Holy Ghost between the ages of 11-13.

I repented, was baptized in Jesus' Name, and received the Holy Ghost when I was 12 years old. I was invited by someone from Powderly Holiness Church in 2007. I made my first visit at that time and later made it my home church.

When Mariah was 2 or 3 years old, she ran a very high fever. A knot appeared on her neck, and she refused to eat for several days. Prayer was made, and God proved Himself to be the Great Physician.

Gaige ran a very high fever and began having seizures. Prayer was made; someone touched God; the fever and seizures stopped.

Presleigh is a very curious child. God has kept her through so many incidents. She has drunk rubbing alcohol, ate the gel out of an opened ice pack, and numerous other things that she placed in her mouth.

About 3 years ago, I had something to attack my body while I worked at Carhartt. I was not able to eat or drink for 2 weeks. I had a hard time swallowing and experienced shortness of breath. This lasted for about 2 months. Prayer was made; God delivered and healed my body.

When April was a child, she had a problem with warts all over her hands. She even went to the doctor and had them burnt off, but could never fully get rid of them. Finally, she went up for prayer. God delivered her from the warts, she is no longer bothered with them.

God kept me from an overdose in the hospital, paid my bills when there wasn't enough money, and delivered my wife in homebirths with our 4 children: Mariah Nikohl, Caleb Gaige, Presleigh Grace, and Monica Jayde.

JOSHUA & APRIL HARDIN FAMILY

Ricky Henderson

I started attending a UPC church in about 1983. I repented, was baptized in Jesus' Name, and received the Holy Ghost in 2000. I met some people from Powderly Holiness Church and started visiting. I made it my home church in 2000.

RICKY HENDERSON

Brandon & Brittney Horn Family

(Brittney) I first started attending Powderly Holiness Church in October 1989. Sometime prior to this, my dad had come to the church to hold a revival. My sister Amie and I came with him. When we started attending the church, my Mom enrolled us in the Powderly Christian School. I started in Kindergarten and graduated from the school.

I repented and was baptized in Jesus' Name in 2006. I received the Holy Ghost when I came up out of the water.

On May 21, 2000, I was bitten by a brown recluse spider four times above my elbow. I broke out in an itchy rash all over my body and began running a fever. The next morning a large bruise appeared on my arm. Later, it developed into four large blisters. I could not stand anything to touch it. It felt as if I was being bitten continuously and I felt an intense burning sensation go through my arm. Infection was raging through my body. I could not sleep or get any relief. This went on for 5 ½ months. I had family members to tell me if I did not seek medical attention that I was going to die. I just told them that Jesus would take care of me.

We were at ladies' prayer meeting one Monday night. Mom said, "It usually eats out and leaves a hole."

Sister Shirley said, "It doesn't have to."

All the sisters gathered around and anointed me with oil just like the Bible commands and began to pray over me.

God showed up! It never ate out. It was a long, wearisome trial; but God proved Himself to be faithful. He carried me through and everything healed up just fine. Jesus is always right on time!

In 2013, my husband had several health issues. He was no longer able to hold a job or provide for our family like he wanted to. For three years, there was no income. God kept us and provided through it all. I would like to share two special incidents from this time period. God not only cares about the big things, but He is also concerned about the small things.

One particular time, as I was going to church, I stopped to check the mail. Our Kentucky Utilities (electric) bill had arrived. It was $500. Remember, no income. My heart sank and I said, "God, you know all about it." I went on to church. As I walked in the door, someone met me and handed me $500. Praise God! He moved before I could even ask Him.

Another time, we needed toilet paper. I had not told anyone except God. I had gone with my brother to help him run an errand. He dropped me off at my house. I heard him honking the horn. I looked out and saw him laughing and pointing at my car. He had stacked a toilet paper tower on the hood trying to be funny. He did not even realize God was providing our needs with a smile. God has been so faithful, always supplying our needs and sometimes our wants. Not one time did a bill go unpaid. God is so good!

The biggest blessing God provided us with is our only child: Nikya Faye Horn.

BRANDON AND BRITTNEY HORN FAMILY

Gary & Diann Joines Family

Gary and I have been blessed with three wonderful children: Danny Ray Joines, Gary Wayne Joines, and Rebecca Danyell Jeffries. We lost Joseph Bryce Joines before he was fully ready.

I was born and raised in church. My dad was the Elder Wilbur Shemwell. I repented in September 1966 and was baptized in 1969 or 1970.

God has been good to us. We are blessed more than we deserve. I was in labor with Danny for 18 hours. I was having a homebirth and began to experience some complications. Someone asked me, "What will you do if you can't have this baby?"

I replied, "I will just lay here and die."

Then the Lord put a song on my heart. I began to sing "Just a Closer Walk with Thee." I was singing while he was being born.

When I was in labor with Rebecca, I was having a homebirth also. Mama was delivering her. Things were going very slow. I was in a lot of pain. Prayer was made, the Holy Ghost would fall; but nothing would change. This happened over and over. Finally, Joyce called Eugene and told him to call Gary. Gary was told to get in there and pray. He was informed that it was possible that both me and the baby could die. When Gary prayed and did what he needed to do, everything changed and Rebecca was born.

GARY AND DIANN JOINES

Jordan & Veronika Lewis Family

We have been blessed with five wonderful children: Kanaan Realous, Mary Karoline, Karmine Jordan, Khoi Abel, and Leigha Kadence.

I first visited Powderly Holiness Church as a child with Sarah Strange and Krystal Lindsey. I was in 5th grade (1998). I remember feeling something I had never felt before. Time went on and we went our separate ways. I was attending college. My mom had repented and was attending the church. God began to deal with me and brought me back home. I repented on December 8, 2007, and was baptized in Jesus' Name about a week later. I received the Holy Ghost on August 17, 2010.

God has been so good to our family. He's been with me during the homebirths of my children. God has answered countless prayers and watched over us so many times when we were unaware of what was happening. I wasn't raised in the holiness way, but I thank God for revealing His truth to me. Most of all I thank God for His mercy.

JORDAN AND VERONIKA FAMILY

Jeff & Kimberly Lovins Family

God has blessed us with a wonderful family. We have 7 children: Jessica (Ben) McIlroy, Andrea Beitz, Grant (Allison) Lovins, Luke Lovins, James Lovins, Elisabeth Lovins, and Tabitha Lovins.

We also have been blessed with 6 grandchildren: Drew, Carter, and Emery McIlroy; Jaxston Lovins; and Emma and Chloe Bunch.

(Kim) I praise the Lord for this beautiful truth! As a child, I never thought much about God or a god. In my ignorance, I entertained my share of Devils. Drugs, alcohol, and one-night stands became the norm for me in my search for something, but "I knew not what I searched for." The morning after my 21st birthday, I woke up on a strange couch in the arms of a strange man I had never seen before and haven't seen since. By the grace of God, this man didn't take advantage of me in my drunken and drug-induced stupor, but rather sheltered me from the prior evening's party. Today, I realize that man must have been an angel sent by my God! By the age of 28, I had been married, divorced, a single mom with two little girls (Jessica and Andie), and expecting my son Matthew "Grant" by the man I am currently married to. I now realize God placed this man in my life to lead me to His Truth. It's amazing how the Lord will use a sinner to get your attention.

I repented on April 11, 1993. I was baptized in Jesus' Name and came out of the water speaking in other tongues. Glory! The Lord began a great work in me! He began to transform me into a child of the King! My life of drugs, alcohol, and promiscuity was over! "I found Jesus. I knew that I would search no more."

By 1997, my husband was preaching the Gospel in Bloomington, Illinois. I was expecting my third son James. The Lord dealt with me about trusting Him with this baby. Brother Larry and Sister Tilda Shemwell, Brother

Keith and Sister Sharon Shemwell, and Sister Rita Findley made the trip to Illinois to deliver our son. My mother, an unbeliever, was there. Things went on for a few days. Then God worked it out that she would need to leave for a camping trip. While she was away, the baby was born. God knows who needs to be a part and how to shelter his children from unbelief.

In 2000, I was privileged to also have a homebirth delivery with Elisabeth. I had called Sister Sharon Shemwell and informed her that the time was right. Brother Larry and Sister Tilda Shemwell were bringing her. They had made it as far as Terre Haute, Indiana, which is about halfway, when Elisabeth decided to make her arrival. Brother Lovins had to take care of the delivery with the assistance of Sister Sharon Shemwell via cell phone. By the time the Shemwells arrived in Illinois, Elisabeth was still full of a lot of fluid. Sister Sharon worked with her and suctioned a lot of it out. She was congested for about 2 weeks. One day, the Lord allowed her to spit up a LOT of that fluid. All was well following that, except for the fact that her eyes were continuously matted. Elder Donald Lance came and preached "Decree a Thing." As prayer was made, Elisabeth's eyes were healed!

The year 2002 came around and I was expecting Tabitha. Brother Lovins had been battling what many people told him were symptoms of appendicitis. Brother Larry, Sister Tilda, Sister Sharon, Sister Rita, and Sister Tina all made a trip back to Illinois. They spent a week while I was in labor. Things seemed to have subsided and they returned to Kentucky. They spent one night at home and had to repeat the 6-hour trip, because things started happening again. Sister Tina couldn't make it that time, but Brother Keith Shemwell returned with them. They arrived to deliver a breech baby. God had blessed us with Tabitha and healed Brother Lovins of his problem! No appendix removed! No C-section! Just God results, because we did it God's way!

With seven children, God has kept His hands on my family. From the times I didn't know about---to the times I did.

Luke (my 4th child) fell in the fire while camping in Florida. We wrapped his hands and prayed. On the way home, we stopped by Brother Tingles in Madisonville, Kentucky. An evangelist happened to be preaching on "trusting God." We, of course, took Luke through the prayer line. After church, Luke tripped and fell on rocks, landing on his hands! We all gasped, but it never bothered Luke at all. He just got up and kept walking! No scars or sensitivity to heat ever followed....JUST HEALING!

Luke also mashed his thumb in a door jam. His thumb was hanging by a piece of flesh. As Brother Lovins prayed, God helped me to slide the tip of his thumb back in place. He has all feeling and mobility in his thumb today.

Jessica flipped her Eagle Talon in a cornfield and walked away with a little scratch on her head.

Elisabeth broke her leg while playing on the trampoline. At seven years old, she chose to trust the Lord. One week later, during worship service, she was determined to get her healing. She laid her crutches down and began to walk around!

On the way home from Arkansas, Tabitha began to cry out from an abscessed tooth. I called Brother Lovins to pray. Within 30 minutes, deliverance came and she never complained of that tooth hurting her again.

Grant broke his collar bone while playing in the barn on his skateboard. We prayed. God healed!

I had what appeared to be a gall bladder attack; but at the Name of Jesus, that had to go.

I could go on telling of the many times God has moved for our family from financial blessings to spiritual upliftings to healings to providing shelter. I thank the Lord for all He has done for my family!

When Jessica was eight, God filled her with the Holy Ghost! When Andie was thirteen, conviction led her to the watery grave to be baptized in the Name of Jesus in the icy river in the middle of February. One night, after church was dismissed, everyone was standing around fellowshiping. I found Andie on the floor speaking in that heavenly language.

When Luke was about five years old, Brother Lovins preached on the "Winds of Pentecost," and that little boy was lost in the Spirit as the other little children went out to play. When Grant was about eight, he insisted Brother Lovins take him out and baptize him in Jesus' Name in the swimming pool.

After we moved to Kentucky, Elisabeth and my three sons repented and received the Holy Ghost, having some extraordinary experiences during a time of revival among the youth at Powderly Holiness Church. At ten years old, God filled Tabitha with the Holy Ghost and she went down in Jesus' Name!

While some of my children have forgotten their first love, I'm believing that the experience they had in their youth will bring them back to His loving arms.

I thank the Lord for Powderly Holiness Church that has lived a life of trusting God before me. It has truly helped to increase my faith through the years in an area where trusting God was not practiced. Since I met the Shemwells, via Sister Sharon Ortiz in 1994, I had always loved what I felt in their services when I would come to visit. Each time I had to leave and return home, I would cry en route. In 2009, the Lord moved us here and made it my home church.

"...And I found Jesus, I knew that I would search no more. He filled that longing down in my soul!"

JEFF AND KIM LOVINS FAMILY

Aaron & Cyndi Morris

We have been blessed with 3 beautiful children: Eric (Ashley) Eaves, Veronika (Jordan) Lewis, and Summer Morris.

We also have 8 grandchildren: Kanaan, Karoline, Karmine, Khoi, and Kadence Lewis; and Abram, Emree, and Remington Eaves.

(Cyndi) I repented and was baptized and received the Holy Ghost in the fall of 2006. Aaron was working night shift. I was feeling very lonely and started visiting the church. God placed me under conviction and saved me.

When Summer was a little over one year old, she got very sick. She developed a bump on her abdomen. It didn't seem like anything to worry about. Before long, it got larger and started running with infection. We were concerned, but calm. As time went on, they started popping up all over her body. It was my first time trusting God. We spent several sleepless nights where she would cry from the pain. It was hard to hold her without hurting her. People began to tell us that it was boils, staph infection, and other things. I was young in God and He spoke a Scripture to my mind. One day, I asked Aaron, "Doesn't the Bible say something about 'where two or three are gathered together in my name, He would be in the midst?'" We agreed and prayed. The next morning, the ones in her diaper area were draining and she received some relief. Praise God, He does answer prayer! From that point on, the places began to heal.

The Lord healed me of a sickness. It lasted about 2 weeks. I thought at times I was going to die. I would beg Aaron to please help me. All he knew to do was to pray. A couple of the brothers from the church came to pray for me—Brother Ryan Morris and Brother Brian Wynn. I was so scared, but God had mercy. Thank you, Jesus! I could go on and on about the things He has done for me and my family. He's been a good God to us!

AARON AND CYNDI MORRIS FAMILY

Brent & Candice Morris Family

We have been blessed with five beautiful daughters and one son: MaKayla, Madison, Macey, Marissa, Mason, and Mayleigh.

(Brent) I was born and raised in the church. I repented and was baptized in Jesus' Name in 1993. I received the Holy Ghost in 1995.

(Candice) I was introduced to the church when I met my husband and we started dating. I repented and was baptized in 1998. I received the Holy Ghost in 1999.

Our greatest miracle was the gift of Salvation.

God has done so many things for our family. I would like to share two special ones. God healed our son of Neisseria spinal meningitis in 2007.

Madison's Miracle
By Brent Morris

Thursday, May 20, 2004, was one of the most devastating days of my life. We gathered at my parents' home on Thursdays for family dinners. As I arrived on this particular day after finishing my work for the day, I saw a little girl approaching the street. She had just gotten off her toy 3-wheeler and was attempting to cross the street. She noticed my brother Chad had gotten his golf cart out to ride and she loved to ride it. As most three-year-olds would do, she crossed the street right into the path of an oncoming car. She walked right into the front fender of the car, which was traveling at an estimated speed of 45 mph. The child was thrown an estimated 72 feet, according to the police report. I saw all of this unfold right before my eyes, unaware that the little girl was my daughter Madison. I parked my truck and walked to where the child landed. As I approached the child, along with my dad and her Aunt Stephanie, I then realized the child was my three-year-old Maddy. We picked her lifeless body up from the blacktop and carried her up the sidewalk to Mom's house. Someone had called 911 and the paramedics had arrived. They began working with her as they loaded her into the ambulance. They took her to the local gas station, where she was airlifted to Vanderbilt Children's Hospital in Nashville, Tennessee. We later learned that one of the paramedics had made the statement, "If she makes it to Vanderbilt before she dies, it will be a miracle."

She arrived at Nashville, still unresponsive and remained in that condition for 4 days. They began running scans and tests to check for internal injuries. After the tests were completed, they found she had one bruised lung, some bleeding on the brain, and minor bruises and scratches.

For every reader's interest, my little girl's nose never bled from the impact, neither had she suffered any broken bones. I consider that alone a miracle.

As the days went by, we were spoken to by many doctors. They informed us there was the possibility she may not remember anything or anybody, including the faces of family members. They said she would probably have to learn to walk again, could suffer brain damage, and could have to learn to do everything again.

I remember the first day she awoke and began to respond to us. I was taking a shower and my wife began to holler. My little girl lay there with her eyes open for the first time in several days. The first thing my wife asked her was, "Do you know who that man is?"

I will never forget as long as I live. My little girl looked up at me and said, "Daddy."

From that day on, things began to improve. In seven days, we brought her home. With lots of prayer from God's people and the mercies of God, our little girl is now 16 years old. She is as normal as any other child and God recently filled her with the Holy Ghost.

God is a miracle working God and nothing is too hard for Him to do. I give Him all the praise!

BRENT AND CANDICE MORRIS FAMILY

Chad & Stephanie Morris Family

Chad & I met after we began attending the church. We started dating in high school while attending Powderly Christian School. We married shortly after graduating. God has blessed us with a wonderful family. Jessica is our only daughter. She is married to Alex Dean and they blessed us with our first granddaughter Ember Skye and our first grandson Hugo Maddox.. We also have three sons: Dustin Wade, Dalton Kent, and Lathan Carter.

All four of our children as well as our granddaughter were delivered in homebirths. My mother is one of the midwives and had the privilege of delivering her first great-grandchild.

(Stephanie) I repented and was baptized in Jesus' Name during the summer of 1988. I received the Holy Ghost the latter part of 1989. Chad repented and was baptized while in the fourth grade. He received the Holy Ghost on December 31, 1991.

I have witnessed many miracles performed during my lifetime, but I would like to share one very special one that was performed in my own home.

On April 9, 2006, God sent us our baby boy, Lathan Carter Morris. He weighed in at a whopping 9 pounds 4 ounces and was 22 inches long. He was my largest baby at delivery. Only God knew what we were getting ready to face. About 2 weeks after he was born, he began throwing up and having fever off and on. He would keep me awake at night. It seemed about 11:00 every night the episodes would begin. Nothing seemed to soothe him. He got to where he would not eat anything. I tried formula and several different kinds of bottles, but he would not take anything. Some people told me he may have thrush. We tried treating thrush, but that didn't help at all. I had prayer for him several times. He just refused to suck anything. My mother came and stayed with me. We began feeding him formula with a dropper in order to get some nourishment into him. He wouldn't take much. All I knew to do was to trust Jesus. God had been there so many times in the past. We were in a church service on May 23, 2006. Lathan was now 6 weeks old and had lost down to about 6 pounds. He looked so bad. Sister Danika Drake began singing a song with the lyrics, "If I could just get in one of those meetings."

Sister Kathy Whitehouse asked me to walk around with Lathan. I felt such opposition, yet I wanted to be obedient. I walked around with him as worship service was going on. I started praising the Lord and the Holy Ghost came down. Instantly, the Lord healed my baby. I was thinking in my mind, "Lord, just give me a peace like you have in the past and I will know it is done."

As soon as I began thinking those thoughts, Sister Shirley Strange walked over to me and said, "Peace I give unto you: not as the world giveth, give I unto you. Let not you heart be troubled; neither let it be afraid." (John 14:27)

I knew it was done! I claimed it that night. That night after church, he started nursing again. He still has a good appetite today. What a GREAT God we serve! Thank you, Jesus!

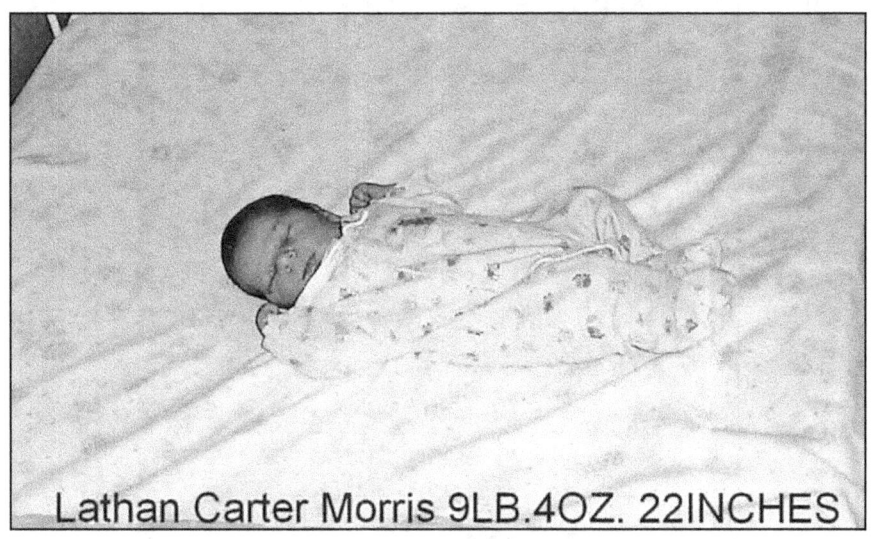

LATHAN MORRIS AT BIRTH

LATHAN WHEN HE WAS NOT ABLE TO EAT

CHAD, STEPHANIE, AND LATHAN

CHAD AND STEPHANIE MORRIS FAMILY

Deborah Morris

I have been blessed with some wonderful children: Steve (Gina) Morris, Terry (Heather) Nunley, Billy Morris, Michael (Misty) Morris, Aaron (Cyndi) Morris, Ryan (Tanya) Morris, Joey (Jackie) Morris, Missy (Tomas) Niave, Alicia Morris, Beth (Kevin) Whitaker, and April (Joshua) Hardin.

I feel as though I could write a book about all that God has done for me—not because I'm more special than anyone, but because He cares for His own. We never have a reason to get down Spiritually. If we would just stop and look down the road to where we began our journey with Jesus, it doesn't take long to remember all He has done. God cares for the large and the small things, because He cares for the things I do. God has never let me down.

One of the first things that comes to mind is when we lived in a house in Moorman, Kentucky. It was a wood-frame house with an upstairs. It was all we had and we had no insurance. One night after church, it was cold outside and I didn't feel like allowing any of the children to sleep upstairs. I couldn't really understand why; I just didn't really want them sleeping there that night. Sometime later in the night, we received a knock on the front door. Someone traveling down Highway 431 had stopped to awaken us to the fact that our house was on fire. They said the upstairs bedroom with the curtain was burning. We got everyone out and I called Mama. I told her, "You have gotten to pray. Our house is on fire! We have no insurance." (We couldn't afford it at the time.) It was all we had to live in. We called 911 and it took awhile for the fire department to arrive. When they finished extinguishing the fire, they were amazed, because it had been several minutes between the time we called and the time they arrived—also taking into account the time it was burning before we were awakened.

What does fire do? It spreads! Well, not this time. They said, "We don't know how, but your house has been burning several minutes in the same spot." They couldn't explain it, but I knew God knew that was all we had. Prayer was made and God moved. In the upstairs bedroom, the bed was scorched and the curtains were burnt; but no one was hurt and we didn't lose our house.

The second thing that comes to mind is when my little boy Aaron was around 2 years old. He was playing in the back room of our home at Moorman. I went to check on him and Ryan, the baby. I noticed Aaron had something in his mouth and was choking. I checked in his mouth, and the object was lodged crossways. I didn't want to move it—afraid I would push it on down. I thought it was plastic. I called Mama to pray. I told her that Aaron had swallowed something, but I wasn't for sure what it was. Aaron was turning splotchy blue and bloody mucus was coming out of his mouth.

Mama lived 7 miles away. When she received the call, she began to pray. She felt like she had touched heaven. Marty, my brother, was bringing her to my house. Marty wanted to drive fast, but Mama told him, "Son, there is no need to speed; everything is going to be okay."

My brother Larry also came. He had first aid training in the mine where he worked. They tried everything their hands could do to help, but to no avail. Larry handed Aaron back to me. He went to the back porch. He took Aaron again. God was just proving man's extremity is God's opportunity. Larry took Aaron one last time. Aaron let out what sounded like a small belch and out came the object. It was a rusty roofing nail.

The next week my brother Ronnie was at work. He worked with someone that had a child that had a piece of plastic lodged sideways and choked to death. God was merciful and allowed me to keep my little boy.

Not long after this, Aaron fell out of a tree and broke his arm. Prayer was made and God healed his arm.

I encountered my first real trial after I repented in 1975. My baby boy Michael was born with raw blisters all over his body. I wanted to trust God. The blisters grew worse everyday. I would pray and then just look at him. I called Mama and Daddy to pray. They both told me, "Give it to God."

I thought I did. But I kept wanting to watch it to see how bad it was or how big the blisters were. But that's not how you trust God. One morning I awoke and the blisters had gotten worse. I called Mama. She told me once again, "You are going to have to give it to God."

Bill went to work that morning. I picked Michael up and began rocking him. I told God, "Lord, if you want him, you can take him here at home while I'm trusting you. You can also take him if I take him to the hospital. You are the life giver. But if you would, I would love to keep my baby a little longer."

I knew God could take him, but I didn't know what he would choose to do. I laid Michael down and sometime later, I went to change and feed him. As I picked him up, I noticed there were no more raw blisters on him. God had healed my baby and let me keep him.

When Ryan was born, the umbilical cord was wound around his neck really bad. He was another of my homebirths. I had my last babies at home after I got in church. My Aunt Edith thought he was dead. He was completely blue all over, except for one small speck of pink on his cheek. They worked and worked with him. They held him upside down and were praying. Finally, God moved and he did not die.

When Ryan was in his teenage years, he and some other boys went to the swimming hole. Ryan was not a good swimmer at all. My sister Vickie called and said that she didn't have a good feeling about their swimming and wanted us to pray. We prayed. My sister Gayle and Susie Balliet were out of town. They knew nothing going on, but felt very impressed to pray for Ryan at this time also. Ryan began to struggle in the water and was too far away to make it back to shore. My son Joey got to him and would go beneath him and push him up to get air. I don't know how many times he did this; but he said the last time he pushed him up, he was getting very tired. God sent an angel. A guy saw what was happening and came and helped Joey. They got Ryan to shore. God moved and was merciful, because Ryan didn't drown that day.

Ryan said he remembered as they tried to get him out, going underwater and swallowing it in an attempt to breathe. His struggles in the water left him weak and as he began going down toward the bottom, the light from the sky began to get blurry and he seemed to be going out.

The Devil still wasn't finished with Ryan. He has been after him since the day he was born. During his high school years, my kids attended the Christian school. Ryan left home, enrolled in the public school and began playing on the basketball team. That was not good enough just to play; but Ryan was good. Here this boy shows up and this team becomes almost unstoppable. Word got out how good he was, and coaches came to town from big universities to scout out Ryan. The Devil had him in the spotlight and was offering him fame and fortune. That's a dangerous place to be. The Devil never shows you the BIG picture, but always blinds the eyes of the souls of men. He doesn't want them to recognize their need of a Savior or to think about where they will spend eternity. Ryan could have gone on a fully paid scholarship to play ball for some well-known universities; but during his senior year, his Grandmother invited him to go to church with her. He promised her he would go, but Grandmother passed away before he found time. He had a sister-in-law that made the comment about "just giving up on him." But God had another plan.

Conviction penetrated the spotlight the Devil had all around him. He visited the church after Grandmother had passed away. God knocked one more time and he answered the call. God called him to preach. Prayer works!

God laid it on my heart to go on a 30-day fast for my children. God began dealing with me, and I began to write their names down in the order God was going to save them. I got to Michael's name and God said, "No, he's not next." I took Michael's name off and wrote another name in his place. Then I wrote Michael's name. God saved all my children in the exact order that I had their names written down.

While giving birth to my son Joey, I went through a major battle. I suffered 5 hours straight—no relief. I didn't have the Holy Ghost, and I battled going to the hospital. My uterus was high and tilted. I wanted to trust God. I didn't want to go to the hospital. While suffering, I would look at each midwife, looking for something to change. Then began the war in my mind. After each contraction, I would say, "I'm going if he isn't born with the next one."

I don't know how many times I did this, but I finally made up my mind. I thought, "If I go to the hospital and die, I will go to hell; because I don't have the Holy Ghost."

The Devil said, "You can go, but it won't cool the flames of hell."

But I also knew, that if I died at home without the Holy Ghost, I would be lost.

When I made up my mind, I said, "No, Devil, it won't cool the flames to trust God at home, but I'm going to go down fighting."

I believe it was 2 contractions later that Joey was born.

When I was expecting Alicia, I had some major health issues. I didn't go to the doctor, but Mama said that she thought it was my gall bladder acting up. I'd hurt severely when I would eat or suffer the pain if I didn't eat.

In June or July of 1986, Terry left home to go live with his dad; and I was in this shape. I didn't eat or drink anything, except water for a whole month. I lost a lot of weight. I never felt Alicia move. Actually, I thought she could have been dead; because I felt no life. As my delivery date came around, Mama would ask me, "Are you hungry?"

One night, I ate one small bite of a cracker and took a sip of grape juice. The next night I ate 2 bites of a cracker and a sip of grape juice. I knew I had no strength to deliver the baby. I told God one morning while folding clothes and listening to the radio, "Lord, would You just let me know that You are going to be with me?"

All of a sudden, a song began to come across the airwaves. I had never heard it before nor since. I can only remember one part of it. It says, "His angels are encamped around you, and they'll keep you from harm."

I knew from that point on, that everything would be alright.

When the time came, I had one pain and it was really hard. But I didn't have another one for a long time. Diann called and then came over. I had another one very hard—but they were very far apart. She called Mama—my midwife. Mama arrived and sometime later, I had another pain. Mama said she was going to call Aunt Edith—the other midwife. I was in denial, because—yes, they were very hard, but so far apart. I had another one lying in the bed and I told Mama, "The baby is coming."

When Mama came into the room, the baby was being born. Alicia weighed 8+ pounds.

Before Alicia turned 2 years old, I developed a large growth and a knot on my abdomen. I did not go to the doctor, but my sister-in-law asked her doctor about me. He explained that I had cancer and would not live to have another baby. I don't know what it was and wasn't looking to find out. Mama went to a youth rally somewhere and asked for prayer. She said that something has gotten to move. I used the restroom one day and the toilet was filled with 100 or more little white balls. I flushed once; they didn't all go down—27 were left behind. I got 3 of them out to show Mama. I have no idea what it was; but God moved, and I have had 2 more babies. I'm still here with all my wonderful children.

God has been good to me. Why would anyone not want to trust Him? He is good and faithful to His children. Jesus let me find my favorite barrette one time. It was my FAVORITE. Yes, I could have gone and bought an entire pack, but I loved that one the best. I prayed and two days later, I found it. I got up at church and praised Him for it, too. He cares for the small things and the big things. If we get discouraged, we need to stop and look around; because He's always there. He's never let me down. I thank and praise Him!

DEBORAH MORRIS & BETH WHITAKER

Donnie & Charlotte Morris Family

(Charlotte) I was born and raised in the church. My husband and I both repented and were baptized in March 1975. I later received the Holy Ghost.

We have been blessed with six wonderful children: Chad, Brent, Lesley, Kendra, and Erica. God saw fit to take our baby daughter Heather home to heaven after delivering me during an ice storm that had hit our county. My last 5 children were all delivered in homebirths. I was attended by midwives in our church.

We have also been blessed with sixteen wonderful grandchildren.

In 2016, God blessed us with our first great-granddaughter: Ember Skye Dean and in 2017 our first great-grandson Hugo Maddox Dean.

DONNIE AND CHARLOTTE MORRIS

Joey & Jackie Morris Family

We have been blessed with five beautiful children: Madden Vines, Paizley Nichole, Nadalee MaCall, Joseph Grayden, and Cortlynn Blair. They were all born in homebirths and delivered by midwives in the church.

(Sister Jackie) I was not raised in the Powderly Holiness Church. I attended the Baptist church as a child probably every time the doors were open. I was active in the church until I was about 16 years old. As I got older, school and sports began to consume my time. If you had asked me if I were a Christian, I would have replied, "Yes." I was taught, "Once saved, always saved," and I was doing all I knew to do. I graduated high school, worked full time, and began attending a community college. I worked for a doctor and planned on becoming an elementary school teacher. That was my goal for life. But God had other plans!

I met my husband when I was 16 years old. His family was quite a contrast to mine. He had 10 siblings; I had one. I noticed the long hair and skirts worn by his family members, but I never bothered asking questions. We dated 4 years. He was presently living with an older brother. His brother and sister-in-law had backslid and were no longer attending church. Their 11-year-old son Steven repented at home during January 2007. I did not know what the word *repent* meant. After Steven's conversion, I began to hear more about church and truth—baptism in the name of Jesus. Steven's mother shared with me that she wanted to go to church to watch how her son would act. I was eager to go with her. The next night we both got ready and went. Needless to say, Misty did not leave like she went. She repented.

I cannot recall everything that transpired during this period of my life. But God was getting ahold of me! The night Misty got baptized, she stepped out on faith and took an extra towel believing that her husband was going to need it that night. It paid off. Her husband Michael walked the aisle that night and was also baptized in Jesus' Name along with his wife. God was still working on me. I was experiencing sleepless nights, losing my focus at work, and thinking about my life and the things I was feeling. I began to lose interest in things and began to lay aside things before I even repented. I didn't realize at the time the changes God was making in me, but looking back, it's undeniable. I had always heard about Heaven and thought that's where you went when you died. Now I began hearing about a place called Hell. At this point, I began visiting Powderly Holiness Church regularly. I came as I was. I began to feel something I had never felt, and I began to feel a longing and a hunger that NOTHING I tried could fill. I knelt down at a metal chair in the old church and cried, but I didn't realize why I was crying. No one made me cry and I couldn't remember what was making me cry. I just remember that as I knelt, I began to say, "I don't know what to do. I don't know what to do. I don't know what to do." I was twenty-two years old and did not know how to pray. I remember preparing for church and didn't know why I was going. I tried to get Joey to go, but he refused. He told me, "I know what is going on. You are under conviction." I would cry to myself all the way to church. Joey stayed home. I would question why I was going and why I was crying, but I didn't know. I walked in the church. People would look at me quizzically as I went and took my seat. One night after church, Joey's brother Ryan came to me and said, "It just came to me. I want us to be together in heaven." I said, "Okay." Then went right on talking to people around me. By and by, Sister Danika Drake came by and started singing that same song, "I Want Us to Be Together in Heaven." I didn't realize that Ryan had been referring to a song. Almost everyone else had exited the church. Sister Danika started singing and I started melting. I cried and buried my face. I tried to pull myself together. I finally opened my eyes and I'll never forget the love I felt. The back of the church and vestibule was filled with people.

In the spring of 2007, we were in the new church and

Joey went with me on a Sunday morning. I can't recall much about the sermon or the singing, but both of us marched down the aisle to the altar. I was crying and kneeling at the altar and crying out, "I'm ready. I'm ready." Although I still didn't know how to pray, my journey had begun. I was baptized in Jesus' Name one week later and received the gift of the Holy Ghost about four months later.

Jesus has kept me mentally, physically, and spiritually since my journey began. One experience that I would like to share involves my fourth child Grayden. It seemed when I would become expecting, I would experience a lot of mind battles. This battle seemed more intense. I had a couple of issues I was dealing with in my body and trusting God. I would pray and pray and still no answer. I kept reminding God that He knows all about it and He's the only one that can fix it. On top of the mental stress, long nights, fear trying to grip my heart, tears that only God understands, I went almost 3 weeks past my due date. I would pray and still no answer, no change, no virtue. I just felt lonely and scared. After my due date, I received a call. The person told me they felt like reading about Jehoshaphat--the time when the enemy was coming in on him. He sought God and reminded God about the things He had done for the children of Israel. God heard and told Jehoshaphat, "Fear not, don't be afraid of the multitude coming against you. Gather up some praisers. The Lord shall fight your battle." As I began to listen to the words of encouragement, the Holy Ghost fell on the phone. It was God, because no one knew how I prayed or knew about my situations. No one but God. The peace of God and faith began to take ahold of me. It wasn't hard to believe God anymore. He had answered so precisely that I knew everything would be okay. The Word had spoken, but everything remained the same for about 3 weeks. The time for delivery came and I chose to praise Jesus. I began to sing, "We've got the victory." The Devil tried to hinder. I couldn't get the song out right, couldn't get it in the right chord, and forgot the words. The enemy began to bombard my mind with thoughts such as, "You are silly. This isn't going to bring deliverance." Jesus said it would, and I just kept on singing the words I could remember and the fiery darts the Devil was sending were all quenched. I began to really feel Jesus after singing for awhile. Things stayed the same, but I felt I had done all God said; and I will never forget that peace. I lay down for a bit and even dozed off. Things began to pick up quickly. The midwives were just telling me to rest. My husband almost missed the baby being born and he was asleep beside me. Jesus delivered Joseph Grayden Morris. He has been my largest baby, weighing in at 10 lb. 7 oz. I felt like he was a trophy. Jesus was so real. Many times we wonder why or what is going to happen. But when the battle is over and the smoke lifts, you look back and it makes the victory sweet. You see where Jesus dropped nuggets and it gives you strength to get to the next place. You can't have the testimony without the test. It gives you hope because you can look back and say, "I remember when." He's been better to me than I deserve. I thank Him for always being there for my family in the small things and big things.

JOEY AND JACKIE MORRIS FAMILY

Michael & Misty Morris Family

(Michael) I was raised in the church. I repented and was baptized in February 2007. I received the Holy Ghost a few years later.

(Misty) I started attending the church in 1989 when Mom enrolled two of my siblings in the Christian school. Michael and I started dating and were later married. I repented on January 24, 2007. My 11-year-old son had repented and I went to church just to see how he would act. God got ahold of me that night. I was baptized in Jesus' Name & received the Holy Ghost that same year.

We have three wonderful children: Steven Michael our only son. We also have two daughters: Stormie Paige and Reese RyAnne.

I had the privilege of having my two daughters in homebirths while being attended by midwives in the church.

MICHAEL AND MISTY MORRIS FAMILY

Ryan & Tanya Morris Family

God has blessed us with nine wonderful children: Robert Cain, Brenna Renae, Eli Coy, Karlie Jean, Ariel Hope, Jeremiah Ryan, and Kirby Lance. Our twin sons Paxton Ryan and Preston Ryan were only allowed to stay with us a few days after their birth. They were all born in homebirths and delivered by midwives in the church.

(Tanya) Ryan was born and raised in the church. The first time I attended Powderly Holiness Church was during the funeral of Ryan's Grandmother "Peggy" Shemwell. This was March of 1998. I repented and was baptized in January 1999.

The Lord has met all of our needs and a lot of our wants. He has been there for every sickness, birth, financial hardship; as well as, spiritual and mental situations when we needed Him. He has protected, healed, hedged in, and sheltered our family. Most of all He has convicted, enlightened, and proved Himself time and again to us and our children.

RYAN AND TANYA MORRIS FAMILY

Lillian Diane Mouser

God has blessed me with three wonderful sons: Anthony, Dewayne, and Jerrid. I have also been blessed with 13 grandchildren.

My granddaughter Lexi has been with me since birth.

I repented in April 1994 in Campbellsville, KY. I was baptized in Jesus' Name in July 1994 and received the Holy Ghost in August 1994.

I met Pastor Larry Shemwell in 1995. He visited the Jesus Name Mission in Campbellsville that I attended. We started fellowshipping with the Powderly Holiness Church. After a few years, my son Anthony began dating Brother Larry's daughter Brittany. They married in 2003.

Eventually, our pastor discontinued fellowship with Brother Larry because of the born again message.

Finally, in 2010, God brought me back to Brother Larry's church. I attended a ladies' meeting that year. My mother had passed away on March 28, 2010, and the ladies' retreat was in April.

I would usually come to get away for a while and to spend time with my son and his family.

By this time, I carried a chip on my shoulder and was very cold in the Lord. On Friday morning of the ladies' retreat, Sister Sharon Shemwell was asked to speak. The title of her message was "You Are Worth a Del Monte." I sat there wondering what pineapple had to do with church and began picking her apart. She read the Scripture in Luke 10 about the Good Samaritan and asked the question, "Who really is your neighbor?" At the closing of her message, she explained why she used the title "You Are Worth a Del Monte."

The following story is her explanation.

You Are Worth a Del Monte
(Shared by Sis. Sharon Shemwell at the
2010 Daughters of Zion Ladies' Retreat)

Brother Gary and Sister Donna Linville started a home missions work in the early years of their ministry. As years passed, they found themselves completely indulged in every area imaginable. They opened a Christian school and daycare. They were both holding down full-time jobs to keep everything operating. They had spread themselves so thin until they were physically and Spiritually drained in about 10 years. Brother Linville resigned the church. They felt like failures and left totally devastated.

Sometime afterward, they attended a conference in California. While attending, they ran into an acquaintance—Brother Nathaniel Pugh—son of J.T. and Bessie Pugh. He wanted to introduce them to his parents. Sister Linville said she and her husband felt so worthless and inferior. Before heading back home to Virginia, Brother and Sister Pugh approached them and asked them to come by Odessa, Texas, to rest for a spell. They were given free lodging in the evangelist quarters. Their original plans were to stay about 6 months. They ended up staying 5-6 years.

One day, not long after their arrival, Sister Pugh called to say she wanted to take Sister Linville to get some groceries. Sister Linville tried to be very conservative in her selections. She placed 2 bananas, 2 apples, a small head of lettuce, and some generic products in the cart. As she reached for a black and white generic can of green beans, Sister Pugh grabbed her hand and said, "Donna, stop that! That kind has all the stems and broken pieces in them. I like Del Monte and you are worth a Del Monte."

Sister Linville fell across her chest weeping. Sister Pugh instructed her to put everything back. She said, "We are starting over. You are worth a Del Monte."

(Sister Diane Mouser) After hearing Sister Linville's testimony, God began dealing with my heart. God told me that I also was worth a Del Monte. I realized God loved me and was there for me. He showed me where I had gone wrong; and that He could and would fix things in my life, if I would totally surrender. The tears flowed freely as I begged God for forgiveness and renewal.

It felt as if I had been cemented in a wall, wanting to be freed, and with no way out. Jesus broke that wall on April 9, 2010. The condemnation was gone. I felt freer than I had all my life. He delivered me that day. Shortly thereafter, I was rebaptized by Brother Ryan Morris at Powderly Holiness Church. This is now my home church.

I moved to Central City, KY, in October 2010, and God has been more real to me than I could have ever imagined. I am now renewed and preaching for Him. I am trying to let people know that even though we stumble and fall, Jesus will pick us up and put us back on the right path if we will allow Him.

SISTER DIANE AND HER SON ANTHONY AT LADIES' RETREAT

DIANE MOUSER AND LEXI

Adrianne Perry

My grandmother June Perry attended Powderly Holiness Church. I first repented in a Baptist church. At the time, I was satisfied and felt good about my lifestyle. In 2012, I attended a tent revival hosted by Powderly Holiness Church. I felt something I had never felt before. I then realized there was more to living for God than what I had been taught. I then began attending Powderly Holiness Church. I repented in 2011 and was baptized in Jesus' Name in 2016.

ADRIANNE PERRY

MY GRANDPARENTS— JUNE AND LUCKY PERRY

Ricky & Teleah Rust Family

(Teleah) God has blessed me with a wonderful family. Ricky & I have six beautiful children: Kali, Tara, Ricky III, Cassidy, Jaxen, and Izayah. I was born and raised in the church. My parents Tony and Deborah Daniel had always taken me. I repented in 1993 and received the Holy Ghost in 1996.

God has done a lot for me and my family. He has touched my children many times when they were sick. He has protected them even when I didn't realize they were in dangerous situations. On May 29, 2006, we had a car accident. The vehicle flipped several times and Ricky was thrown out. I am very thankful to God that He showed mercy. Ricky was hurt, but it could have been a lot worse. The children and I only had a few scratches and bruises. I know God was watching over us that day. If it wasn't for His love and mercy, I don't know where I would be today.

RICKY AND TELEAH RUST

RICKY AND TELEAH RUST FAMILY

Chris & Penny Saylor Family

(Chris) Penny and I started dating in the summer of 1994. We visited the church a few times before I repented. I repented, was baptized in Jesus' Name, and received the Holy Ghost in September 1995. I backslid in December 1999, but rededicated my life to God in December 2001.

In the latter part of my teenage years, I was plagued with a physical condition. The doctors diagnosed me with a type of seizures. When they occurred, it was frightening. I couldn't move any part of my body. I couldn't talk. It seemed as if I were paralyzed. The only thing I was able to do was to hear and to see. I was hospitalized on three different occasions. I was told that the dilantin level in my body was zero. I started taking Dilantin medication on a daily basis to prevent these episodes from occurring. The doctors explained to me that I could never stop taking the medication or the seizures would reoccur. The Devil is a liar! The night I went to the altar, I stopped taking the Dilantin. I have not taken it for twenty-two years, neither have I had any more episodes. God did not just forgive me of my sins; He also healed my body. Praise you, Jesus, for your healing power!

(Penny) I was born and raised in the church. I repented in December 1995 and was baptized in Jesus' Name the following March.

One night during a church service, Brother Nathan Shemwell felt led to get a pan of water. He asked if there were any women that wanted a baby. If so, he asked them to put their hands in the water. I was one of the women. I placed my hands in the water and soon after found out I was expecting. About 4 months later, I began having some complications and things weren't looking good. It was during this time that God prompted me to read Joshua 1. He comforted me with these words: "I will not fail thee nor forsake thee. Be strong and of a good courage; be not afraid, neither be thou dismayed: for the Lord thy God is with thee." One month before our seventh anniversary, I delivered our son Clay in a homebirth. He tipped the scales at 10 pounds. Thank you, Jesus, for the blessings you have given us.

When Clay was older, he was on his way to feed the dogs one afternoon after Chris had left for work. I was in the front yard when he came running and yelling, "I stepped on a snake!"

I walked down to where he had stepped on the snake and saw that it was a copperhead. I sent him after the shovel. In the meantime, I kept my eyes on the snake. It lay there very still as if it was dead. I thought maybe it was. When he came back with the shovel, I determined I had to make my first thrust at the snake count. When I jabbed him with the shovel, he was very much alive! Thank you, Jesus, for your hand of protection! We serve an awesome God!

"He's an on-time, God, yes He is!"

COPPERHEAD SNAKE THAT CLAY STEPPED ON

CHRIS AND PENNY SAYLOR FAMILY

Brandon & Sandy Shemwell Family

The Lord has blessed us with two beautiful daughters: Gracie & Emma.

(Sandy) Brandon was born and raised in the church. I first came to Powderly Holiness Church at 12 years old with neighbors and have been coming ever since. None of my family attends, except for my sister Pam.

My first experience in the church was repentance and baptism in the winter of 1994. I received the Holy Ghost February 15, 2015.

I can say that our family has truly been blessed! Jesus has been with us through the thick and the thin. He has always supplied our needs as well as our wants at times. He has healed our sick bodies, put money in our pockets when we needed it, paid bills for us, repaired our vehicles, and raised up our youngest daughter Emma when she was near death. Her fever had gotten so high that she lost most of her hair, yet Jesus gave her a beautiful head of NEW hair! Jesus has never let us down.

*Editor's note: Sandy was also one of the barren women that obeyed and placed her hands in the bowl of water. She also became expecting very soon and delivered Gracie not long after.

BRANDON AND SANDY SHEMWELL FAMILY

Derek & Jenny Shemwell Family

We have been blessed with four wonderful children: MaKenna, Derek Jr., Cameron, and Shyleigh.

In January 2012, we found out we were expecting our fourth baby. It had been six years since our last baby and we were overly excited.

In early April, there were some complications that arose; and by the middle of June, we knew that we were having a baby girl with major health issues.

The first problem was a duodenal atresia. This is a complete closure of the duodenum. At that time, the doctor told us it is ONLY caused by one of two things: Downs Syndrome or Edwards Disease. He asked if termination of the baby was an option. I was horrified that he asked and immediately said, "NO!"

He looked at me very sternly and said, "You had better hope it is Downs Syndrome, because Edwards Disease is a total vegetable state of being with absolutely no quality of life."

Again, I was horrified.

The second problem he said we were being faced with was Hypoplastic Left Heart Syndrome (HLHS). The left side of the heart is either not there or is very narrow and the blood will not flow through normally. He said there were a series of three open-heart surgeries that would have to be done, in order for her to live. The first surgery would be conducted immediately after birth, the second within seven months, and the third usually around two years old. He gave us a survival rate of 20%, and it would be a long, heart-breaking journey. He explained that there are only 1 in every 100,000 babies born with this heart defect, and it is the rarest and most complicated heart defect.

At this point, we are asking, "Why us?" This is supposed to happen to other people—people we only hear about—NOT us! We were in complete shock! In just a matter of minutes, our lives had drastically changed.

As the months passed, I kept expecting, when I would make my doctor's visits, that he would come in and tell me that they had made a huge mistake and our baby was just fine. That's how I was expecting God to change things. There were several people praying for "God's Will." I was just praying for a miracle like I wanted it. God has a way of showing you that He is in control, and His ways are not our ways. I had to learn this the hard way.

Shyleigh was born on September 29, 2012, weighing 7 pounds 12 ounces. She looked absolutely perfect! No Downs Syndrome or Edwards Disease. However, they took her immediately for tests, and informed us that she still had a blockage and HLHS. She would need her surgeries after all. Our baby was going to die if we did not do the heart surgery. You know the Devil has a way of getting what he wants, and he knows how to trick you.

Before she was born, and when we had found out about her problems, I had asked God to let me know that everything was going to be alright. I asked God to let someone who knew nothing about our situation to just come to me and let me know that everything was going to be fine. A few weeks later, Brother Michael Morris came up to Derek and me after church had dismissed and said, "I feel like God told me to tell you that everything is going to be okay." There was my confirmation! Thank you, Jesus! But, like I said, the Devil can trick you, if you are not careful. He did just that.

Right after Shyleigh was born, and they confirmed their diagnosis, "the Devil" in the form of a little woman doctor walked into my room. She stood at my bed and cried and pleaded with me to give Shyleigh a chance. She convinced me that she needed the surgery. She said, "Her heart is in better condition than most babies with this diagnosis, and the surgery will not be as invasive for her. She will not need the open-heart surgery. We can go in from her side, and do one little surgery, and she will be fine." LIE!! We believed her.

She also had another plan up her sleeve. She let us know that if we did not sign the paper to allow the heart surgery, they would not do the surgery on the blockage; therefore, Shyleigh would not be fed, because the food would not pass through her system. We were given an ultimatum: sign papers for surgery OR starve your baby! So we agreed.

At two days old, they performed the surgery to get rid of the blockage (which wasn't a blockage at all). It was only a webbing that would have allowed food to pass through. No wonder there were no signs of Down Syndrome or Edwards Disease. Following this surgery, we were faced with several things. One doctor tried to convince us to just let her go. She was having issues with her heart rate being too high; she would stop breathing and turn blue, even with the ventilator in. We were so confused. I just couldn't lose my baby. This was on a Tuesday evening. Our family was called in and rushed to be with us. Before 8:00 that afternoon, Danika called and requested the church to pray. At 8:00, her heart rate went back to normal, she didn't stop breathing anymore, and started doing good.

At eight days old, she had her first open-heart surgery. We were now convinced that we had been lied to by the little lady doctor. We were going through with the open-heart surgeries. The first one lasted about 4 ½ hours. They said she did extremely well. Little did we know—we had a long journey ahead. She went on ECKMO (life support for babies). She was on 15 medications, including adult dosages of pain medications. After a period of time, she became addicted to these. We were not able to hold her until she was 2 months old. We could only sit and watch. We watched her heart beat for 7 days with an open chest to allow the swelling to subside. We watched her being kept alive by machines for several weeks. We also watched her die several times. Through all of this, God was right there. He never left us. While we were at Kosair Children's Hospital in Louisville, Kentucky, we saw so many children die. We often wondered if we were the next family to have to go through it.

We were there for 10 weeks 2 days. We had to walk away from our home, the only way of life we had known, and our other 3 children. It was the most traumatic experience we had ever had to face. I believe that God placed us in that situation to teach Derek and me that we had to learn to lean on Him. We also had to rely on one another. Since that time, many things have changed in our lives.

The doctors told us all the "gloom and doom" that we would face. They said, without a doubt, that Shyleigh would always look blue, have low oxygen levels, stay tired, would remain on multiple medications, and never be an active child.

SHYLEIGH IN HOSPITAL

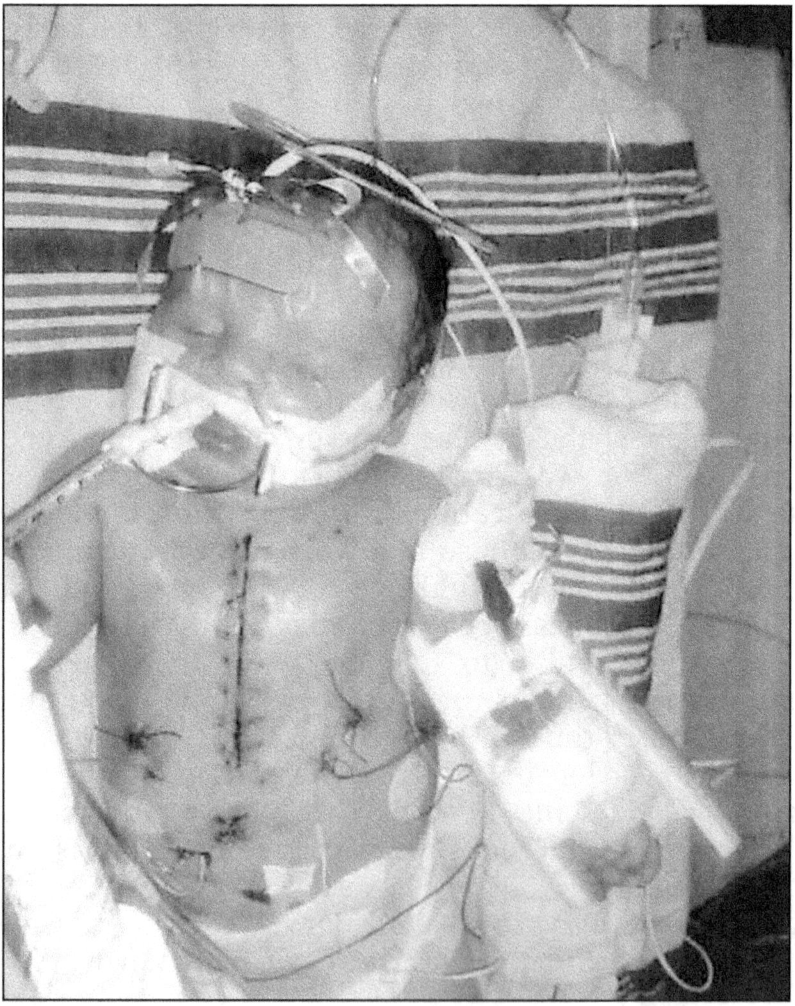

Yes, she was blue and had low oxygen levels, until her second open-heart surgery in April 2013. Following that surgery, her complexion changed completely. She looks completely normal now. Her oxygen levels are in the high 90s. She NEVER gets tired and is very active. I don't think she ever slows down. She has been free from medication since May 2014! The third open-heart surgery is no longer required! Thank you, Jesus! The doctors are amazed and say that it is impossible, but I know that with God, all things are possible!

We are so thankful that God allowed us to keep our baby girl. She is truly a walking miracle! Although things did not happen the way that I wanted or expected them to, God was there, and the church family was there. God showed us that He will always be there right on time!

SHYLEIGH

Janae Shemwell

I was taken to church all my life. I previously repented, was baptized, and received the Holy Ghost in 2014.

In the summer of 2014, God spared my mom from death.

After walking away from the house of God, God's love and mercy allowed me to come back and be restored.

JANAE SHEMWELL

MY MOM—SISTER DEBBIE SHEMWELL

Jason & Christy Shemwell Family

We have been blessed with 3 children: Noah, Jaden, and Madison.

(Christy) I met Penny Shemwell (who later turned out to be my sister-in-law) at the Ponderosa and was introduced to the Apostolic way. We both worked there. Penny was a light to me. She was so meek and humble and a really sweet girl. I would watch her and just be in amazement with her countenance. I was raised Baptist and never knew the truth. We were taught "it's okay to sin; you just ask for forgiveness." Jason was raised holiness. We met in 1994 at Ponderosa. I knew when I met him that he was a really good guy. We married in 1997. We lived a worldly lifestyle while we were having our children and raising them. That lifestyle almost destroyed our marriage. We were into drugs and alcohol and on the verge of getting a divorce. We were invited to church in 2011. Jesus saved our marriage in 2011 and our home in 2012. Jason repented April 17, 2011. I repented May 1, 2011. The children repented soon after. I received the Holy Ghost on July 5, 2011. My daughter Madison received the Holy Ghost on January 29, 2017, while in the 6th grade.

Jason got sick in 2016. He had a very high fever for about 2 weeks. He was unable to walk. But he decided to trust God and God delivered him!

Noah was healed from an issue of blood in 2011. God came by right on time!

We have been healed of many sicknesses and God has moved for us in many times of need. He is an on-time God. God will never leave us nor forsake us. He is the Great I AM!

JASON AND CHRISTY SHEMWELL FAMILY

Jeremy & Christy Shemwell Family

(Jeremy) I was born to Pastor Larry and Tilda Shemwell during the great revival of 1976. I gave my heart to Jesus at the age of 12 years old and received the Holy Ghost on January 17, 1995. Christy and I were introduced at Long John Silver's in Central City, by my cousin Hudson Perry, in November 1993. She worked with some of our church members. She was a member of Reservoir Hill Pentecostal Church. We started talking and married on August 11, 1995. From that union, God has blessed us with 3 wonderful children: DaKota (1996), Trevor (1997), and Candra (2000). We had the pleasure of trusting Jesus and experiencing a homebirth with our daughter. Our first grandchild Riley was born in 2017.

On March 30, 2011, God chose to bless us again, when Hayden Gary Nathaniel Benson was placed in our home. He came into our home at the age of 4 months and has been with us for 6 years. He has brought such a joy that we would be lost without him.

God has definitely been good to us. Our children have never missed a single day of school due to sickness. God has blessed us in many ways. We have received financial blessings to meet needs and have received healings in our home. God healed me of a spider bite by a brown recluse spider. I trusted God through it all and He delivered.

Joshua & Brandi Shemwell Family

God has blessed us with seven beautiful children: Zachery Keith, Daryl Kent, Jacquelin Nicole, Kelli Elizabeth, Cameron Drew, Kaci Brooke, and Gavin Ray.

(Joshua) I was born and raised in the church, but that did not make me a Christian. I repented the time we used the blue and white tent for our first tent revival on September 22, 1993. One miracle I recall is when Jackie was very young, she developed a bad dairy intolerance. She would forcefully throw up anytime she ate or drank any dairy product. Sister Dianne Pulse was in town preaching. There was a prayer line. I spoke in Jackie's ear that God would heal her. She had prayer and was instantly healed.

(Brandi) I first came to the church in January 1995. I came from Michigan with my friend Kari and her family. We eventually moved to Kentucky. Sometime after this my foster mother repented and enrolled us in the Christian school. I repented in July 1995 and was baptized sometime later. I received the Holy Ghost in August 1997.

All seven of my children were born in homebirths. I was attended by midwives in the church. God delivered me with all of them. One of the greatest trials I went through was in January and February 2012. Gavin was about 1 ½ years old when he developed a knot about the size of a billiard ball on his neck. He was so sick. We feared losing him. This went on for a couple of weeks. He even stopped wanting to eat or drink. One night, I happened to be home alone with Gavin. Joshua was out of town for a job. The kids were asleep. Gavin was motionless and his lips started turning blue. All I remember is crying and praying. I said, "God, he is yours. If You want to take him, I give him to You." A peace came over me and right then I determined whatever God decided to do, I would be okay. If God had decided to take him, I knew he would be with Jesus. Nevertheless, if I got to keep him, I would rejoice. Sometime later, the place on his neck opened up and started draining. In days, he was fine. God allowed me to keep him. He turned 7 years old in August 2017. Through that trial, God became MY God.

In 2016, Zachery fell and hurt his tailbone really bad. Through it all, he chose to trust God and God delivered him. My God is an awesome God!

Zachery works for the Central City Fire Department. In February 2017, he received a call to a house fire. While at the scene, he fell 14 feet off a ladder and all he received was a sprained ankle. I know God was watching over him!

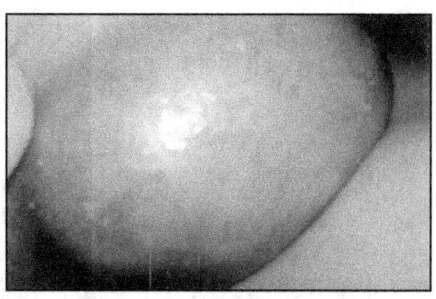

GAVIN WITH KNOT ON NECK

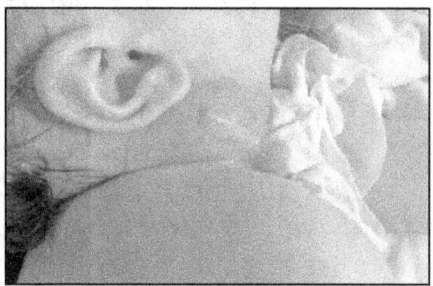

JOSHUA AND BRANDI SHEMWELL FAMILY

Justin & Jordan Shemwell Family

(Jordan) Justin was born and raised in the church. His dad has been his pastor all his life. He repented on July 2, 2000; he was baptized the following night; and received the Holy Ghost the next night.

I was taken to church all my life by my parents. We had previously attended the Crossing Holiness Church. I started attending Powderly Holiness Church when Justin and I started dating. I first repented and received the Holy Ghost at 13 years old and rededicated my life to God when I was 15 years old.

I had an affliction in my body for about 17 months. It seemed like nothing I tried to do for it would help. It would improve for a week or two; then get worse again. My mind was in constant torment. I had several people to tell me how serious it was. I was told I needed to go to the doctor and that it would be easy to fix. I had witnessed many miracles in our home as a child growing up. Mom and Dad trusted God for everything. My mom had delivered me and my siblings in homebirths. I wanted to trust God about my situation, but I did not have a peace about it.

After dealing with this for about 16 months, Sister George from Jonesboro, Arkansas, happened to be at the church holding a revival. She was preaching about how the three Hebrew children had a made up mind to serve God. No matter what they had to endure, they were going to trust God. After she preached that message, I got a peace about my situation. I told God, "It doesn't matter what the outcome is. I'm going to trust You."

In two weeks, things began to improve. A month later, I was completely healed. God knows how to teach us to trust Him, if we are willing to walk through the fire.

We had been married a few years and Justin had changed jobs. He took a $4 per hour pay reduction, but we felt like that was what he should do. During that time, God taught us about depending on Him. A couple of people gave us money during this time. They had no clue about our situation or needs. Once we had taxes due, and I kept trying to add up the bills. I kept trying to figure and refigure to make it work. Justin told me not to add it up again. He said, "We are going to pray about it and leave it alone." That's what we did. When the time came to pay the taxes, somehow the money was there. God is always right on time!

JUSTIN AND JORDAN

Keith & Sharon Shemwell Family

We have been blessed with 6 wonderful children: Shannon (Gigi) Shemwell, Joshua (Brandi) Shemwell, Kimberly (Jason) Wilson, Keisha Shemwell, Nathan (Tiffany) Shemwell, and Virginia (Steven) Burris.

God has also given us 24 grandchildren: Chelsea & Justin Gibson; Zachery Keith, Daryl Kent, Jacquelin Nicole, Kelli Elizabeth, Cameron Drew, Kaci Brooke, and Gavin Ray Shemwell; Dustin (Paige) Wilson; Phillip Ervin, Jason Luke, Jayla Shawnee, Jonathon Seth, and Nolan Keith Wilson; Denver Sky, Dallas Waters, Durango Lands Shemwell, and Hunter Aiden Mejia; Tristan Nathaniel, Trenton Matthew, Diamond Leigh, and Julianna Shemwell; and Ian Miles Burris.

We were blessed with our first great-grandson in May 2016: Roman Abel Wilson.

(Sharon) I was not raised in the church. My Grandpa Phillip Uzzle was pastor of the Pentecostal Church of Jesus Christ in Hartford, KY. We would attend Sunday School there occasionally, but I was never really brought up in church. When I was about 7 or 8, my siblings and I began to walk to Nelson Pentecostal Church for Sunday School. We absolutely LOVED going to church! We would line up on the first pew, grab a songbook, and sing along with everyone in congregational singing. I learned many of the old hymns from those days. I remember the first time I felt conviction. We were attending a gospel singing at the same church. The singers were "The Roy Loney Singers." They sang "The Apple Tree Song" that night. I remember feeling like crying and wanting to go kneel at the altar, but I had no clue why I was feeling that way. Later, my mom repented and started attending Powderly Holiness Church. I was about 10 years old. I was taught many things about holiness and living a godly life. I repented in November 1974 during a revival with Brother Charles Clark. I was only 13 years old. I attended a public school and the Devil had lied and told me that if I lived for God, I would not have any friends. My mom was already in the church. So I was not allowed to do many worldly things. After repenting, I returned to school with such a boldness. I was never ashamed of my Jesus. I would carry my Bible to school with me and if God prompted me, I would share with my peers. I was baptized in Jesus' Name on December 8, 1974. It was snowing and very COLD! I was baptized in Broadway Pond at Centertown, KY. I received the Holy Ghost in May 1976.

Keith repented and was baptized in February 1975. He received the Holy Ghost several years later.

KEITH AND SHARON SHEMWELL

God has proved Himself as the Great Protector in many situations in our lives. Keith has worked as a welder/fabricator for 34 years. He builds large sawmill equipment. Approximately 30 years ago, he was painting a gang saw that had been finished that week. This particular machine weighs about 10,000 pounds. The machine was being held off the floor by an overhead crane to allow him to paint the bottom. At one point, he was standing underneath the machine painting. The Lord spoke to him and told him to get out from under the machine. He stepped out from underneath the machine and it immediately fell, coming from within inches of the floor. Had he not obeyed the voice of the Lord, he would have been crushed and killed.

THIS IS THE TYPE SAW KEITH WAS PAINTING. HAD IT NOT BEEN FOR GOD'S MERCIES AND PRAYER, HE WOULD HAVE BEEN CRUSHED.

Another time, he was using a punch press. He was placing a 9/16-inch by 1-inch die into the press. He started talking to one of his co-workers, not realizing the dies were not properly aligned. His co-worker John Clapacs was breaking a piece of metal on the opposite side of the machine. John asked him, "Are you ready?"

Keith replied, "Yes."

Keith pushed the button. The dies were crossed. The machine sheared the die and immediately shot him in the chest. It sounded like a rifle going off. Keith didn't realize at the time what had happened.

He thought he would play with John. He grabbed his chest and told him he had been shot. John responded, "No, you weren't."

About that time, Keith looked down and saw a hole in his shirt. Then he began to get scared. He unbuttoned his shirt and saw his chest covered in blood. He felt on his chest but couldn't find anything. Then he thought it must have gone inside. As he ran his hand back up his chest, he barely felt the tip of the piece of metal. He pulled it out. It was the die.

When he arrived home that afternoon, he informed me that he had been shot at work that day. I said, "No, you weren't."

He was adamant that he had been shot and showed me the bloody shirt. Then he told me the story. I asked him what time the incident occurred. He said about 1:30.

God had spoken to me at about that time or a little earlier that day to go pray. I was busy with housework and cooking supper and tried to brush it off until later. But I felt a strong urgency to go pray. Thank God I obeyed! I had no idea who or what I was praying for. I just began to intreat God for everything that came to my mind.

When Keith told me the time it had happened, I began to relate to him what had happened to me that day.

David Ford told him, "Your wife was probably praying for you."

Sure enough that was what was happening! It always pays to obey God!

Keith suffered from a malady when he was in the sixth grade. He had gone to his Grandmother's one day in December 1967. His mother had gone to town to buy the boys some cowboy boots. Keith took off for the house. As he crossed his Uncle Gilmon's yard, he felt a pain in his ankle that felt like a mosquito bite.

Before his mother arrived home, his ankle had swollen so big he couldn't even put the boots on. The pain that started in the one ankle moved to the other ankle. Then it left his ankles and moved to one knee then the other. From there, it moved to one wrist; then the other wrist. It next moved to his elbows. When it moved to his shoulders, the pain was so intense, he could hardly move. It also affected his chest at this time. The pain moved from joint to joint throughout his body continuously for 3 months.

During this time, his dad preached trusting God for healing. Keith heard his parents discuss whether to take him to the doctor. They left the decision up to him. He chose to stay at home.

While he was bedfast, his mother held him throughout the night many nights. She never complained, but instead prayed for him, as he watched the moon cross the sky.

God healed him and he was able to return to school that spring. He never suffered any after effects. Many people diagnosed him with polio or rheumatic fever. But regardless of what it was, God is still the Great Physician.

I have a very special miracle that God did for me. We had a 1983 Chevrolet Caprice station wagon when our children were small. It was my means of transportation back and forth to school as I worked in the school. The car began having some problems. The engine would start missing really bad. Of course, I tried to convince Keith to get it checked out and repaired. His brother Lonnie was a mechanic for a dealership at Madisonville at the time. He called Lonnie. Lonnie drove it to work that weekend and checked it out but could not find the problem. He replaced a spark plug, but it began fouling out before he made it back to Central City. I was very agitated about everything and wanted something done NOW. Lonnie said he had no idea, but he would tear into the engine the next weekend. I did NOT want to wait a week. But sometimes God makes us wait, so he can show a greater miracle. That weekend at church, I went up and asked for a prayer cloth to place in the glovebox. The car ran perfectly for that next entire week. No misses or anything. Had it not been for Lonnie's plans to check it out, I would have forgotten about getting anything done. But, nevertheless, we took it for him to see what he could find out. Keith went to help him. As he began to tear everything down, he removed the distributor cap and found a large hole in the very center (see picture below). The car should not have even been running. Lonnie wanted Keith to call me. He began to speak to me and said, "Sis, you've been running on faith all week. That car should not have been running. It's impossible."

I said, "I know. There's a prayer cloth in the glove box."

He said, "You don't understand."

I said, "I don't have to understand, but I still believe."

He encouraged me to keep that distributor cap as a trophy of the miracle God had performed for me. God made me wait an additional week so he could show His Providence and power to me.

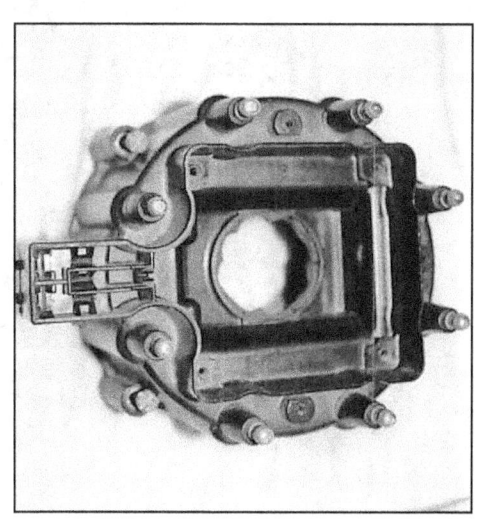

DISTRIBUTOR CAP

Logan Kyle Shemwell

I was born and raised in the church.
I repented in March 2015 and was baptized in April 2015.

Although I was raised in the church, I decided to go out and try the world. But I never forgot my upbringing and the things I had been taught by my parents. I never tried hard drugs or anything such as that. The night I repented the worldly desires were gone. The best decision I ever made in my life was when I surrendered and gave my heart to God.

LOGAN SHEMWELL

Nathan & Tiffany Shemwell Family

We have been blessed with 4 beautiful children: Tristan Nathaniel, Trenton Matthew, Diamond Leigh, and Julianna Nicole.

(Nathan) I had attended Powderly Holiness Church all my life. Tiffany and I met at a youth camp in Martinsville, Indiana. She was living in Murphysboro, Illinois at the time. We lived in Illinois the first few years of our marriage; then relocated to Kentucky.

NATHAN AND TIFFANY SHEMWELL FAMILY

Tabatha Shemwell

I am the daughter of Ronnie and Debra Shemwell.
I was raised in the church, but became saved in 2006.

First of all, I want to say that God has healed my body many times. He has taught me through many trials and tears that I only need Him to see me through.

The first year after I repented, God started testing me; although I couldn't see it at the time. Although I was raised in the church, I did not understand Spiritual warfare. For two years, I didn't know what I was facing. Now as I look back, I can see where Jesus was carrying me through those dark valleys. I never understood when someone would say, "Hindsight is better than foresight." It truly is better. I can now see where Jesus wanted me to trust Him and Him alone. I'm so grateful today and I thank God for real true love.

TABATHA SHEMWELL

Mike Sigers

We were blessed with 3 wonderful sons: Mikie, Timothy (Bo), and Shawn.

We also have 6 grandchildren: Brittany, Kayla, Michael, Landon, Stetson, Chris, and Karisa.

I repented and was baptized in Jesus' Name on September 13, 1981. I received the Holy Ghost on November 11, 1981.

Sister Becky had repented prior to my conversion. She was planning on being baptized on September 13, 1981, following the Homecoming service at the Crossing Holiness Church. Her mother encouraged her to step out on faith and to take 2 towels. She always felt like she would never survive spiritually without my living right. I knew nothing about the extra towel. During the service that day, God began to place me under conviction. I walked the aisle while service was going on and gave my heart to God. Of course, we needed both towels that day as we both were baptized in Jesus' Name.

My wife and I began attending Powderly Holiness Church in 1984. I began to experience an intense hunger for God and felt a need to be fed more and a desire to draw closer to Him.

I have personally witnessed God's hand move in so many ways during my Christian walk. God healed my broken leg, healed both of my injured knees, and my back all without medical intervention. God also delivered me from a toothache that lasted an entire week.

The medical profession says that a person can only live 24 hours when your intestines burst and drain inside of you; yet God allowed my wife Sister Becky to live over 4 years in that condition with no medical help or assistance. It was only by His mercy and prayer. We fully trusted God and He alone decided when it was time for her to go.

MIKE AND BECKY SIGERS FAMILY

BECKY AND SHARON ORTIZ (HER SISTER)
AND SISTER LINDA KYZAR

Timmy (Bo) & Tammy Sigers Family

We've been blessed with 3 wonderful children: Ashley Gay (deceased), Landon, and Stetson.

(Tammy) I was born and raised in the church. I repented at 15-years-old in 1986, was baptized in Jesus' Name in 1988, and received the Holy Ghost in 1996.

Bo had formerly attended the Crossing Holiness Church. He started attending the Powderly Holiness Church in 1984. He repented at 11-years-old in 1982, was baptized in Jesus' Name in 1984, and received the Holy Ghost in 1991.

In 1991, Bo was working at an aluminum plant. One night, the furnace blew up in his face and knocked him about 10 feet back. He went into shock because of the burn and pain. He was taken to the hospital. While in the ER, they were putting ice packs on his face; and the heat from his injury was immediately melting the ice. The doctors came in and talked to us about sending him to a burn center. I was pregnant with our first child, and I didn't want for him to have to go off to a burn center. My Grandmother Shemwell, my mother (Shirley Strange), and my mother-in-law and father-in-law (Mike & Becky Sigers) were there with us. When the doctor informed us that Bo would need to go to a burn center, all we knew to do was pray. My Grandmother Shemwell started speaking in tongues. Bo quit shaking, came out of shock, and went to sleep. He slept all night and came home the next morning. You cannot even tell that his face was ever burnt.

A few weeks after Bo was sent home, we went out to see his mom and dad. Sister Becky was cooking and we were talking. I remember telling Sister Becky I would do anything in the world to have both my mom and my daddy in church. My mom was in church, but my daddy would not allow her to go to church. When I made that statement, Sister Becky turned around and pointed a wooden spoon at me and said, "Tammy, don't ever say that again! God will take the closest thing to you."

I just looked at her and said, "Becky, I really would give anything to have Mom and Daddy truly in church."

As we were talking, Sister Becky asked me, "Tammy, if anything should happen while you are in labor, what do you want us to do?"

There was a dear old sister in the church---Sister Opal Gray—that would come to church so sick that people would have to help her in the church. I would see her go up for prayer. She would get to dancing around and speaking in tongues. She was always okay after that. I told Sister Becky to have Sister Opal to come pray and everything would be fine. Little did I know things were going to turn really ugly!

The night I went into labor, my Grandmother Shemwell was next to death. The family had been called in and I was at her house when I went into labor. Grandmother and Sister Edith Flener were the ones who delivered me and were the midwives all of my life. They suggested I go next door to Sister Edith's to deliver the baby. I believe that trusting God is the only way and a homebirth it would be.

I was in labor for a week. Complications set in. I started having seizures and went unconscious. Brother Larry and Sister Tilda Shemwell talked to Bo about what he wanted to do. Bo had to decide, since I was unconscious. Bo decided we would trust God. That is all we knew to do. Sister Tilda said that she felt like everything would be alright.

Some of my family members turned me in to the authorities. So it was out of our hands at that point. I was unconscious and was taken to the hospital. Grandmother Shemwell was sick and not able to be there. Sister Edith was not well either, and Sister Opal Gray passed away the night before I was taken to the hospital.

Bo and my family got the news the baby was dead, and I wouldn't make it. Someone called the church and told the bad news, "The baby is dead, and they have given Tammy up to die." There was no hope. Someone at the church felt like marching around seven times; then on the seventh time, everyone was supposed to start praising God. The church came together in unity and obeyed.

My baby girl Ashley Gay Sigers was a stillborn, I was in ICU for three days, but God was still doing a great work. The baby was born on Saturday night. My mom was set free to go to church on Tuesday night. I was sent home a week later to die. They declared I would not be able to have any more children. That's just like the Devil—always gloom and doom and bad news. Twenty-five years later, I'm still in church; I have received the Holy Ghost; and have given birth to two sons. My dad Frank Strange repented, was baptized in Jesus' Name, and received the Holy Ghost. Yes, we lost our baby girl, but the good that came out of it was worth everything we had to go through. God took my baby, but in return gave me my mom and dad.

BO AND TAMMY SIGERS

LANDON AND STETSON SIGERS

Peggy & Thomas Stevens Family

We have been blessed with a wonderful family: Blade, Dawson, Varina, and Joseph Stevens, and Austin Lacefield. We were blessed with our first grandchild in 2017: Kayden James Lacefield.

(Peggy) I was raised in the church. I repented and was baptized in July 1979 and received the Holy Ghost that same year.

When Varina was one year old, she became very sick. Her breathing was so bad, she sounded like a dog barking. I was up day and night with her. She lost weight. One night she was so bad that I called and texted Sister Deanna Drake. She was at the Crossing Holiness Church. They were having youth service. Hannah just happened to look at her mom's phone, and noticed I had called and texted. Sister Deanna, Brother Larry, Sister Tilda, and Sister Shirley left church and came and prayed for Varina. Before they got there, I went to my bedroom and had a talk with Jesus. I told Him through tears, "Jesus, I love my baby girl and I want to keep her, but there she is. If You want her, You can take her." I gave her to Jesus that night. After they prayed, her breathing improved. But the battle wasn't over. A few days passed and she became worse. I was up day and night again. Around 4:00 one morning, I was sitting on the couch with her in my arms and I fell asleep. I was so exhausted. I awoke suddenly and looked down at her and discovered she wasn't breathing. I cried out, "Jesus!" Then I screamed at my husband. He never awakens easily, but that morning he came running and took her. When he lifted her up, she made a little sound and started breathing again. I called Sister Deanna. She came over immediately. That same morning about 10:00, I got a phone call from my oldest brother who lived out of state. He said if I didn't take her to the doctor by that evening, he was calling the law. Shortly after, my youngest brother called and said the same thing. I called Brother Larry and relayed what was going on. He asked, "What are you going to do?"

I said, "Trust God." From that point on, Varina became better each day. The law was never called. Jesus healed my baby girl, and she is still with us nine years later. Trusting God for healing still works! All praise and honor goes to Jesus for the stripes He took at the whipping post.

MY MOM—SISTER SHIRLEY STRANGE

Spencer VanMeter

I started attending Powderly Holiness Church in 2012, because I enjoyed what I felt. I repented on October 22, 2015 during school. I was attending Powderly Christian School at the time. God began to put me under conviction. One day, I went to the sanctuary and repented of my sins. I was baptized in Jesus' Name two days later and received the Holy Ghost on October 28, 2015.

God healed my mom of her thyroid problems.

I had been separated from my siblings due to a divorce between my parents. My mom requested prayer everywhere she went that God would allow her to be reconnected with her children. She was not even allowed visitation rights. But God gloriously answered that prayer and brought my older brother back home. My brother has now repented and been baptized in Jesus' Name. God also put it in my older sister's mind to start contacting the family. My mom was allowed to enjoy being a part of her first granddaughter's life when my sister had a baby girl.

God was also with me when I was involved in an accident and broke my nose.

SPENCER VANMETER

Jerry & Kathy Whitehouse Family

We were blessed with 12 wonderful children: Jordan, Jerry III, Devan, Megan, Karissa, Josiah, Katie Rae, Kody, Weston, Nathan, Jon, and Kenzie.

We also have 16 grandchildren: Jacie, Ashlynn, Jate, Dylan, Isaac, Maura, Zeke, Madeline, Quinton, Branson, Houston, Benton, Myleigh, Haven, Kaebree, and Vincent.

(Kathy) Jerry repented, was baptized in Jesus' Name, and received the Holy Ghost in October 1984.

I repented and was baptized in November 1984. I received the Holy Ghost in January 1985.

"Twins with Different Birthdays"
(Kathy)

My labor began with my twin boys around 8:00 A.M. on Monday, February 12, 1996. Normally, I had quick labors; but this one was totally different. I never realized I was having twins, because I planned on having a homebirth the same way I had with all my deliveries. I never had any medical visits, ultrasounds, or anything of the sort. I labored all day. We had many visitors and people praying. The evening wore on and still no baby. Sister Peggy Shemwell (the elder midwife) told my husband there were problems, but we chose to trust God. "It is better to trust in the Lord than to put confidence in man." (Psalms 118:8) The first baby was finally born at 10:34 P.M. Weston Jedidiah Whitehouse weighed in at 9 pounds 8 ounces. He was born feet first. The next baby did not arrive until the next morning at 12:20 A.M. Nathan Uriah Whitehouse weighed in at 9 pounds and was also born feet first. They were both healthy and God delivered us one more time. I had some major complications afterward, but I will let my husband tell "his" story.

(Jerry) After the twins were born, the placenta failed to pass. All we knew to do was to trust in the Lord. After several days, anything man could have done with his hands was gone. We were facing a potentially life and death situation. Sister Sharon Shemwell had called Brother John Scheel at Beebe, Arkansas, to ask for prayer and to inquire if they had ever faced a similar situation during homebirths. He called me back to make sure I understood the consequences of what could happen. I reiterated that all we knew to do was to trust in God.

After several days, I was standing at the bar in the kitchen and telling the Lord, "You have to move this. We need to see this pass."

God spoke to me and said, "I can move this without you seeing it."

I said, "Good enough"

And that's exactly what He did.

Bless the Name of the Lord!

JERRY AND KATHY WHITEHOUSE'S FAMILY

Josiah & Kristi Whitehouse Family

(Kristi) I was born and raised in the church. I repented and was baptized in Jesus' name as a child and received the Holy Ghost in my teenage years.

On March 10, 2010, God gave us one of the best miracles in the world—our baby girl Madeline Brooke weighing in at 8 pounds 4 ounces. This was my first delivery and she was born in a very short time. Everything went well as God planned. On May 26, 2011, God gave us another wonderful miracle---our son Quinton Josiah. He weighed in at 7 pounds 6 ounces. We had the privilege to experience the blessing of having them delivered in homebirths. They were delivered by midwives in the church. They have brought such happiness to our lives! Both of the miracles were brought into this world like God planned. I'm so thankful for the plan of God!

JOSIAH AND KRISTI WHITEHOUSE'S FAMILY

J. T. & Ashley Whitehouse Family

(JT) We had previously attended the church my great-grandmother Sister Edith Flener had pastored—the Crossing Holiness Church. We started attending Powderly Holiness Church in 2002. I repented on November 27, 2005, received the Holy Ghost 2 nights later, and was baptized in Jesus' Name in December 2005.

(Ashley) I was born and raised in the church. My dad has been my pastor all my life. I repented and was baptized in 1998. I received the Holy Ghost on November 3, 2003.

God delivered me in childbirth at home with all seven of my children. They are Jacie, Ashlynn, Jate, Dylan, Isaac, Maura, and Ezekiel.

When Jacie was eleven months old, she ran a fever for two weeks and was sick for a total of two months. She had just started to walk, but lost her strength, and could hardly do anything. One night at church, someone asked me to walk around with Jacie and praise God. While we were walking, someone else stopped me and prayed for her. From then on, things turned around and everything was alright.

J T AND ASHLEY WHITEHOUSE'S FAMILY

Karissa Whitehouse

I had been taken to church my entire life. I had previously attended the Crossing Holiness Church. We left that church and didn't have a home church for a year. We had visited Powderly Holiness Church at different times during my life. We made it our home church in 2002. I repented, was baptized in Jesus' Name, and received the Holy Ghost when I was 8 years old.

I have been a Sunday School teacher for 10 years. I love teaching children.

In October 2016, I became very ill. I had extreme difficulty breathing. I remained very sick for about 2 weeks. Many days and nights I was unable to sleep. I got so weak that I was unable to walk. I had to be carried to the restroom. Someone stayed with me at all times. The saints of God prayed, someone touched God, and He delivered once again! God has proved Himself faithful time and again. I was raised in a home with eleven siblings. My mom and dad practiced trusting God for everything. I have witnessed many miracles in my life.

KARISSA WHITEHOUSE

Kody & Autumn Whitehouse Family

We have been blessed with an adorable baby boy: Dakota Vincent Whitehouse. We are expecting our second child in early 2018.

(Autumn) I was born and raised in the church. My parents had taken me since birth. I repented, was baptized, and received the Holy Ghost in December 2012.

As a child, I was raised and taught to trust in God for my healing. Mom and Dad left the church for awhile, but the teachings I received never left me. I can remember, as a young girl, getting boils that covered several parts of my body for about 6 weeks. Jesus came through and healed me.

When I was seven months along in my first pregnancy, I was leaving church and my heel caught on the hem of my skirt. Before I realized what had happened, I found myself lying on my stomach. I had fallen off the church porch. Instantly, the Devil started attacking my mind. As everyone gathered around and prayed, I knew everything was going to be okay. About 6 weeks later, God blessed us with a healthy baby boy! Being able to experience for myself God's power in delivery through a homebirth, showed me that not only did I need God for myself but also for my baby.

I'm thankful for the mercy God has shown me through my lifetime, because without God's mercy I wouldn't be where I am today.

(Kody) My parents had taken me to church all my life. I and all my eleven siblings were all homebirth babies. My parents lived and taught me about trusting God for everything.

I repented on February 18, 2008 and received the Holy Ghost on October 11, 2015.

Looking back on my life, I thank God for keeping me as a teenager and child. I could always tell you right from wrong. But until I was 19, and got an experience for myself, He was only Dad's God. When I repented, He became my God also.

I work in an underground mine. God has protected me so many times. There have been times that had it not been for God's warning and protection, I would not be alive today.

KODY AND AUTUMN WHITEHOUSE'S FAMILY

Megan Whitehouse

I had been taken to church my entire life. I had previously attended the Crossing Holiness Church. While attending that church, I repented one Sunday morning in the Kindergarten Sunday School class. I was 5 or 6 years old. I was baptized in Jesus' Name one week later. I later received the Holy Ghost during a revival held by Brother Gerald Hicks at the Crossing Holiness Church.

My dad started attending the Powderly Holiness Church in May 2002. I was 14 years old. We also started attending the Powderly Christian School. I have been here ever since.

MEGAN WHITEHOUSE

Jason & Kimberly Wilson Family

We have been blessed with 6 children: Dustin (Paige), Phillip, Luke, Jayla, Seth, and Nolan. Our first grandchild Roman Abel was born in 2016.

(Jason) The good Lord had mercy on me, a backslider, to whom God revealed His truth to me in 1996. I first heard of the Acts 2:38 plan of salvation and many infallible truths at this time. Truly I experienced a life changing event and would never turn loose of what God revealed to me, for it is truly undeniable. The mercies of God were extended to me once again on January 24, 2007, when I repented and rededicated my life to God. Soon after, I was rebaptized and refilled with the Holy Ghost. It's been almost 11 years that God has held my hand and kept me from many dangers. He has also delivered me from drugs and alcohol, an addiction I was once bound by. Many prayers, testimonies, and miracles I have seen and experienced in my walk with God. He has restored my broken family. God has proved Himself faithful to me through many hardships and deaths of family members. In 2016, God saved my son Luke from death. He had many close calls as he battled a chiari malformation. He went through a very serious surgery, but prior to the surgery he was airlifted to Vanderbilt Children's Hospital more than one time and almost died in their emergency room after arrival. God has blessed me with a wonderful pastor, ministers, family, and friends. My desire is to see Jesus with a smile on His face one day.

JASON AND KIMBERLY WILSON'S FAMILY
WHILE LUKE WAS IN VANDERBILT CHILDREN'S HOSPITAL

Brian & Devan Wynn Family

God has blessed us with 3 boys and 3 girls: Branson Lee, Houston Duran, Benton Drake, Myleigh Blair, Haven Montana, and Kaebree Ann. They were all delivered in homebirths.

(Devan) I repented and was baptized in Jesus' Name as a child. I had always been taken to church by my parents. I received the Holy Ghost when I was ten years old.

Brian was invited to church by his friend Ricky Jeffries. God placed him under Holy Ghost arrest. He repented and started attending the church in 2004. He was baptized in Jesus' Name in 2005 and received the Holy Ghost on October 15, 2006.

God was with me during the deliveries of all my children. He is a faithful God!

BRIAN AND DEVAN WYNN'S FAMILY

Anthony & Brittany Young Family

God has blessed us with 8 sons and 1 daughter: Conner, Carson, Collin, Chandler, Carver, Cade, Lily, Cooper, and Cohen.

(Brittany) I was taken to church my entire life. I received the Holy Ghost on March 8, 1998. God has been with me through nine homebirth deliveries. I did experience some minor complications with a few, but God saw me through it every time.

ANTHONY AND BRITTANY YOUNG'S FAMILY

Kenneth & Karen Zguro Family

When we first married, we were not able to have children, but later God saw fit to bless us with three beautiful daughters and one adorable son in 2017. Our daughters are Johnna Rae, Vicki Kaitlyn, and Summer Grace. Our son is Kenneth Blaize.

(Karen) I was born and raised in the church. I repented when I was eleven and received the Holy Ghost in September 1984.

When I was 8 years old, I was run over by a car. The tire was on my back and the car dragged me down the driveway. The church came and prayed after they got me out from under the car. I was able to go to church that night. I never had any problems, because prayer was made and God touched me.

THE ZGURO KIDS

Jesus Name House of Prayer

Sister Evelyn (Shepherd) Abbott had been an acquaintance of the Shemwell family for years. It had been awhile since they had been in touch. Pastor Larry Shemwell ran into her at a funeral and was reconnected. She told him that she had started a work in Sonora, Kentucky, in an old store front building and invited him to come. He had told me about meeting her and I never forgot about it. One Sunday afternoon, I approached him about going to see her. We decided to go that very night. This was approximately 1996. Brother Shemwell, my husband Keith, my son Joshua, and I went to the Jesus' Name House of Prayer that night. It was a very small old building right in the heart of Sonora, Kentucky. Just a handful of people were there, yet we had a very good time in the Lord that night.

From that night, we began a continuing fellowship with the saints in Sonora. Sister Abbott continued to pastor the church until her husband passed away. At that time, she turned the work over to Sister Tina Wheeler. They eventually built a new church in Upton, Kentucky. We continue to fellowship the Upton church on a monthly basis.

SISTER ABBOTT

SISTER TINA

Crossing Holiness Church

The roots of the Shemwell family began in the Crossing Holiness Church. It was pastored by Sister Edith Flener for several years before her decease. It is currently pastored by her daughter Sister Linda Whitehouse. We continue to fellowship this church on a monthly basis. Youth services are rotated among Powderly Holiness, Crossing Holiness, and the Upton church the last Friday of every month.

SISTER LINDA WHITEHOUSE

Sunday School

Children, children, oh, the joy of children! If there's anything we have an abundance of, it's definitely children. We love and adore our children. They are the church of tomorrow. We started a Sunday School program in the early 1970s not long after the church began. It would be impossible to list all the teachers that have been a part of this outreach for the past 40 plus years. Our children have benefited greatly from having this asset in the church. We currently have about 150 children from ages 2-18 enrolled in the Sunday School program. Brother Keith Drake has been the Superintendent for several years.

BROTHER KEITH DRAKE

SUNDAY SCHOOL DRIVE WINNERS FROM 2001: PHILLIP WILSON, ZACHERY SHEMWELL, AND KATIE DANIEL.

SUNDAY SCHOOL CELEBRATION

Powderly Christian School

Powderly Christian School began in 1983 after careful consideration to ensure our children would receive a Christian education. Brother Michael Anderson was our first principal. He carried us through the first year and did an outstanding job!

Pastor Larry Shemwell followed up the second year. He and Sister Tilda Shemwell completed the next 20 years.

Following Sister Tilda's retirement, Sister Peggy Lacefield filled this role for the next 3 years.

In 2007, Sister Sharon Shemwell became principal and is still fulfilling this role at the time this book goes to print.

We currently enroll about 78 students. The school includes grades K-12. The school has always used the ABeka curriculum. We have a great faculty consisting of 12 full-time teachers, 2 full-time custodians, 2 full-time nursery helpers, and several substitutes. With the class of 2017, we have graduated 100 students.

God has blessed us with the school. We have chapel services twice per week. We have witnessed children repenting of their sins, receiving the Holy Ghost, loving to sing for Jesus, and learning about the Word of God.

FIRST YEAR OF SCHOOL WITH BRO MIKE ANDERSON 1983-84

SISTER TILDA PRESENTING CLASS OF 1995 GRADUATE SHANNON SHEMWELL HIS DIPLOMA.

SISTER TILDA SHEMWELL C. 1997

SISTER SHARON SHEMWELL

Bible School

The church has an annual Bible school program during one week in the summer. Brother Chris Saylor is the director of this outreach. Bible school started in 2012. The 2017 Bible school had a total enrollment of 158 children from ages 2-18.

We have seen many children and families that do not attend church to be blessed by this program.

BROTHER CHRIS SAYLOR AND KARISSA WHITEHOUSE.

BIBLE SCHOOL

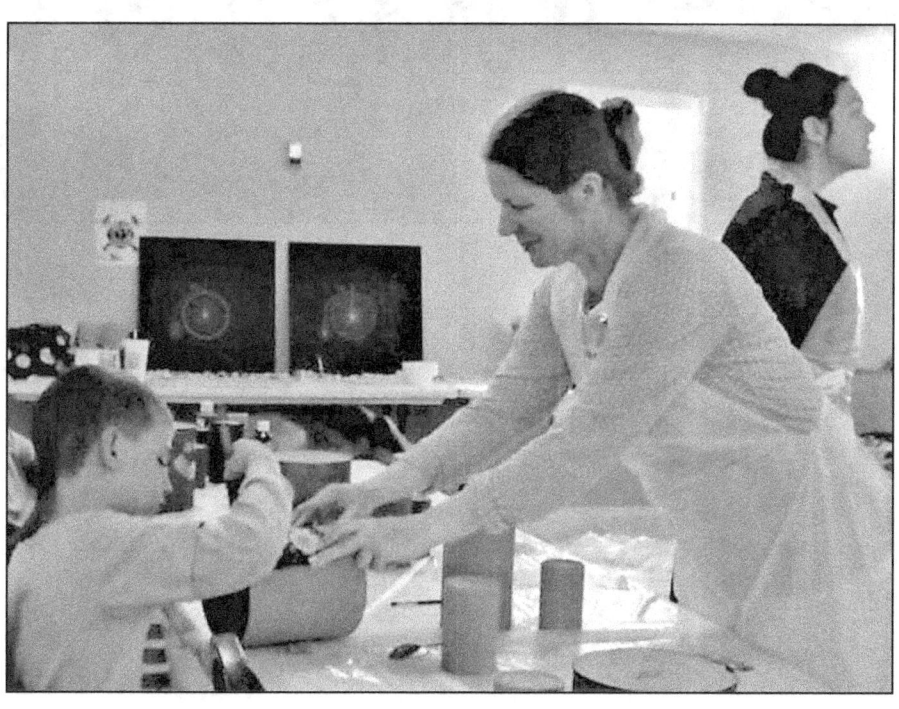

Tent Revival

We began having tent revivals in the fall of 1991. Our first tent revival was held in South Carrollton. We borrowed a tent for the first 2 years. We then decided to purchase our own tent in 1993. We received a $1000 down payment on the tent from a sister in the church. Offerings were taken up to help purchase the tent. We ended up purchasing a 40x60 tent for about $9000.

During the tent revival of 1996 at Brewer Machine, in Central City, we had 2 brothers to arrive. They were acquaintances from years gone by. They actually ended up spending Saturday night in the tent. They were offered lodging elsewhere, but chose to stay in the tent. Our children have never forgotten their song that begins with: "I'm a little mudpie, the apple of His eye...."

We were having tent revival in Powderly, KY, in 2004, when a storm came up. The storm was completely unexpected. We drove to church in sunshine and as soon as service began, straight-line winds began and within minutes the tent collapsed. It was just a miracle everyone got out with no serious injuries. Sister Linda Kyzar was with us during this tent revival.

Brother Frank Strange repented during the tent revival of 2000. He had been a hard-core person that seemed like the last person you would expect to surrender to God. His wife was at the tent and they lived within hearing distance of where it was set up that year. As church started, he began to venture near the tent. He wanted to remain out of sight and was going to stay on the railroad track up above the tent. Some sisters agreed and prayed that God would bring him underneath the tent. God sent the mosquitoes so thick that he couldn't stand them. He began walking toward the tent and didn't stop until he made his way to the altar and gave his heart to God. God made a fine saint out of him. He was definitely a changed man!

FRANK STRANGE'S FAMILY

BELOW: SHIRLEY & FRANK STRANGE

We have had quite a few ministers to preach for us during our tent revivals. Some of them include Sister Lavada George, Sister Linda Kyzar, Brother Gerald Hicks, Brother Archie Owens, and Brother Madison Drew.

BROTHER SHEMWELL PREACHING AT TENT REVIVAL 2017

BROTHER MADISON DREW (TENT REVIVAL)

BELOW: BROTHER ARCHIE OWENS (TENT REVIVAL)

SISTER LINDA KYZAR (TENT REVIVAL)

We won Sister Carol Byars to the church as a result of the tent revival of 2013. She came and sat in the vehicle on the side of the road with her daughter and listened. God put his hook in her and began to reel her in. She and her family have been a tremendous blessing to the church.

TODD AND CAROL BYARS

Ladies' Retreats

We began hosting ladies' retreats in 1998 under the leadership of Sister Deanna Drake. We were privileged to have Sister Ethel Daniel with us as a speaker our first year. Elder Sister "Peggy" Shemwell had always wanted to meet Sister Daniel, but had never had the opportunity. They were able to meet during this retreat. I had the wonderful privilege of having Brother & Sister Daniel to stay in my home. The retreat was on March 13-14, 1998. Sister Shemwell's last service was on Sunday, March 15, 1998. She suffered a stroke the weekend following the ladies' retreat and passed away on March 24 of that same year. God has a way of bringing things full circle that we could never plan.

We have had many wonderful ladies' retreats with a lot of time and effort put into them. We are thankful for the seventeen years that we were able to enjoy the fellowship with many different women. Some of the women that have preached during these retreats were Sister Ford from Florida; Sister Deborah Burris from Southport, NC; Sister Dianne Pulse from Beebe, AR; Sister Linda Kyzar from Beebe, AR; Sister Susan Templet missionary to Ecuador; Sister Janice Alvear missionary to Brazil; Sister Sharon Crossno from Big Sandy, TN; and others.

We never had a bad retreat, but everyone was special in its own way. We are also thankful to all the brothers in the church who have cooked many meals and provided an enjoyable time of fellowship for us.

SISTER COOK AND SISTER ALVEAR

BELOW:
SISTER DEANNA DRAKE GIVING QUILT TO SISTER PULSE

SISTER GEORGE AND SISTER VICKIE KELLER

BELOW: LADIES' RETREAT

DEANNA DRAKE AND PEGGY STEVENS

BELOW: SISTER JEAN AND SISTER BECKY SIGERS

SISTER SHARON ORTIZ AND SISTER TINA WHEELER

SISTER GEORGE

Friends

God has blessed us with many friends throughout the years. The following pages include only a small percentage of those that chose to congratulate the church for this milestone.

Sister Dianne Pulse
Beebe, Arkansas

I was never acquainted with the first pastor and his wife of Powderly Holiness Church. I was privileged to meet Pastor Larry Shemwell, Sister Tilda Shemwell, and the church family several years ago. I have enjoyed their sweet friendship and their constant support of my ministry through the years. This church family has a love for preaching and worship. Pastor Shemwell and his wife are so compassionate in their love for God's people. Their leadership shows in the congregation's giving, love, support, compassion, and fellowship. Congratulations on 50 years of serving the Lord to some of my dearest friends....I love you all!!

SISTER DIANNE PULSE

Sister Deborah Burris
Southport, North Carolina

I was so fortunate to meet the Powderly Holiness Church family several years ago. This church stands for true holiness. The statement I make so often about the church is: "This church proves you can hold a high holiness standard and have a large church." Powderly Holiness Church is one of the largest Apostolic churches I know and has a wonderful holiness standard. I have found this church to be some of the friendliest people I know. Pastor Larry Shemwell would go to the end of the world to help anyone in any way. I thank God for the "Trust God" message they still stand for. I have witnessed them tested and tried and they stood tall and strong. My life has been made richer by meeting this great church. They live what they preach. God bless you for 50 years of dedicated service to God.

SISTER DEBORAH BURRIS

Brother Raul & Sister Janice Alvear
Missionaries to Brazil
Maceio, Brazil, South America

We pray that God will always bless and the church will continue to grow and grow and many souls will be added to the kingdom of God. Thank you, Brother and Sister Shemwell, for your hard work, for your faithful life through the years, for being steady people, always right there serving God.

We, as missionaries, know that we have friends at Powderly Holiness Church, that back us, that love us, that hold up our hands, and we hope we've done the same for all the folks there.

May God bless you all!!

BROTHER AND SISTER ALVEAR

SISTER ALVEAR MINISTERING

Sister Susan Templet
President
Ecuador Missions, Inc.
Puyo, Pastaza, Ecuador

Congratulations to Powderly Holiness Church on 50 years of preaching the Gospel! What an accomplishment and what a great blessing for your city to have had the Truth preached there for so many years! I express my most sincere happiness and also give honor to Pastor and Sister Shemwell for being such wonderful leaders of this beautiful church. I rejoice with you all in celebrating this Jubilee! May the Lord Jesus continue to pour out His Spirit upon this church and may many more souls be won to the Kingdom because of the light y'all shine so brightly for Jesus! God bless you all, Powderly Holiness Church! Congratulations!

SISTER SUSAN

Reverend Charles Madison Drew
Southport, North Carolina

When I think of Powderly Holiness Church, one word comes to mind---Friendship. We've known Pastor and Sister Shemwell and the church family since about 2005. We have had a long-lasting relationship. I know that if I need anything or need to talk, I can call Pastor Shemwell; and if I need advice, he will tell me the truth, whether I like it or not. That's true friendship. I love each and everyone of you and continue to pray for you! Congratulations on 50 years!

BROTHER MADISON DREW

Sister Sharon Crossno
Pastor of Landmark Pentecostal Church
Big Sandy, Tennessee

Dear Brother Larry and Sister Tilda Shemwell
And the Powderly Holiness Church family:

Warmest greetings in the great name of Jesus!

As I sat down to write this note, so many warm thoughts concerning PHC filled my mind. I began to reminisce about the ladies' retreats and special services that I had been privileged to attend. The opportunities to minister God's Word, pray in the altar, and fellowship with you fine folks was such a blessing.

Your assembly serves as a beacon of hope to your community, a light to the lost, and a place of strength to the saints.

What a milestone for the church and pastor as you prepare to celebrate Brother Shemwell's 40 years as pastor and PHC's golden anniversary. May God's richest blessings rest on you as you continue to serve Him!

SISTER TILDA SHEMWELL & SISTER SHARON CROSSNO

Elder Donald Lance
Evangelist and Missionary
Jayess, Mississippi

We were first privileged to meet Brother Lance in 1976. He proved himself to be a faithful friend and blessed our assembly many times with his endtime messages and faith ministry.

Brother Lance made it a point to share many messages through the years in cassette form.

We were sad to hear about his passing on July 24, 2013; although, it was a blessing to attend and share in his homegoing celebration in Jackson, Tennessee. He made an indelible impression upon our saints.

Below are some of Brother Lance's sayings that made us all laugh.

- I will never forget old what's his name.
- Devasticated warthog.
- That person has more problems than a giraffe with a sore throat.
- If you want something done right, do it yourself.
- Some people live and learn. Others just live.
- Blow it. You blew your money when you bought it!
- May your armpits be infested with the fleas of a thousand camels.
- That varmint....
- If they had brains, they'd be dangerous.
- Don't feel like the Lone Ranger.
- That foxed faced devil.
- Think and surprise us all.
- Satan Claus.

ELDER DONALD LANCE

Reverend Linda Kyzar
Beebe, Arkansas

Reverend Linda Kyzar was born in Jayess, Mississippi. She received the Holy Ghost on January 13, 1966. She felt the call of God in her life at the age of 13. At the age of 25, Sister Kyzar quit selling life insurance, and gave her life over to full time ministry. She evangelized for several years, pastored various churches in Illinois and Tennessee. She also did missionary work in the Arctic Circle at the North Pole. She was the founder of MAWP---Ministerial Alliance of Women Preachers. Her desire was to extend a hand of support with friendly encouragement to women who sincerely wanted to work for God.

Sister Kyzar ministered in our church many times---ladies' retreat, Mother's Day banquet, revivals, tent meetings, etc. I was privileged to make a room in my home for her to call her own. She was a tremendous blessing to the church the times she spent with us.

Our prayers are extended to Sister Kyzar at this time. We are so thankful that during this season of her life that God has placed her in an area where she has the love and support of a wonderful church family.

SISTER KYZAR

Sister Lavada Lois George
Missionary and Evangelist
Jonesboro, Arkansas

Lavada Lois George was born on August 7, 1935, in Walnut Ridge, Arkansas. While growing up, she did not have an opportunity to go to high school; but later in life, she earned her high school diploma and five college degrees through Lighthouse Christian College. She wrote several publications for school and college study materials. She also spoke at many school and church conventions. She had a passion for missions, especially traveling to the Philippines, Brazil, Paraguay, and Jamaica. She sent tracts and Bible lessons to more than a hundred nations. Throughout her career, she was a school teacher, principal, pastor's wife, and secretary for the Apostolic Independent Missions. She was mother to eleven children and more than twenty foster children throughout her life.

We were privileged to first hear Sister George minister in 1976 in Hartford, Kentucky. Later in life, she began visiting the church and ministering on an annual basis. She was a speaker at one of our ladies' retreats and taught many times on family life. We always enjoyed the times we were able to spend with her. It was a joy to take her shopping at the thrift shops and Goodwills. I had the privilege to keep her in my home on numerous occasions.

She was one of the greatest soulwinners I have ever met. I have personally witnessed her speaking to backsliders while the tears flowed.

We were saddened to hear of her abrupt passing on June 30, 2016; yet we were allowed to be a part of her homegoing celebration.

She will always hold a special place in our hearts. I know if she were still here, she would make it a point to share in this Jubilee with us!

SISTER LAVADA GEORGE

The Lighthouse
Pentecostal Jesus Name Church

P. O. Box 940
Beebe, Arkansas 72012
www.lighthouse.edu
E-Mail: keeper@lighthouse.edu

Telephone:
Schools 501-882-6210
Church 501-882-3933
       800-548-3988
Fax: 501-882-5257

Dr. John Scheel
Pastor

Rev. Jason Scheel
Assistant Pastor

It is with humility that I write this greeting to the honor of Pastor Larry Shemwell. He has been the pastor of the Powderly Holiness Church, Powderly, Kentucky, for over forty years. This is to be commended.

In spite of personal illness and death of family he has gone right on preaching and ministering to his people.

I commend him for his steadfastness and perseverance in spite of all to carry on the work of God! Not many are willing or able to carry such a load and burden for their flock like this in the 21st century.

Sincerely,

John F. Scheel, Ph.D.

John F. Scheel, Ph.D.

Central Arkansas   The Nations of the World

"... among whom you shine as lights in the world." Phil. 2: 15

DR. JOHN SCHEEL

MITCH McCONNELL
KENTUCKY

United States Senate
MAJORITY LEADER
WASHINGTON, D.C. 20510

September 6, 2017

Powderly Holiness Church
c/o Larry Shemwell
36 Phillip Uzzle Lane
Central City, Kentucky 42330-5132

Dear Friends:

Please allow me to congratulate you and your family on the 50th anniversary since the founding of Powderly Holiness Church. Your joy in this wonderful achievement serves as an inspiration to us all.

Your longstanding commitment to God and community is to be commended. You have my very best wishes as you continue your commitment of sharing your worship service with the community.

Sincerely,

MITCH McCONNELL
UNITED STATES SENATOR

MM/aw

Congratulations!

Commonwealth of Kentucky
HOUSE OF REPRESENTATIVES

District Office
P.O. Box 411
Greenville, Kentucky 42345
State Message Line:
800-372-7181 Ext. 686

Capitol Annex
702 Capitol Avenue, Suite 413
Frankfort, Kentucky 40601
(502) 564-8100 Ext. 686
melinda.prunty@lrc.ky.gov

Melinda Gibbons Prunty
15th Legislative District

September 19, 2017

Powderly Apostolic Holiness Church
4197 US 62 E
Central City, KY 42330

Dear Members and Leadership of Powderly Apostolic Holiness Church,

It is my distinct honor and privilege to write to commend and affirm your church on the occasion of your 50th Anniversary Celebration. Your contributions to our local community have not gone unnoticed. Your members are exemplary citizens and your witness of faith in Muhlenberg County is much appreciated.

Many blessings on your next 50 years! If I can ever be of service to you and your members please do not hesitate to ask. I will do what I can.

Respectfully,

Melinda

Rep. Melinda Gibbons Prunty
15th Legislative District

Committees
Health & Family Services - Vice Chair • Education • Small Business & IT • Medicaid Oversight & Advisory

REPRESENTATIVE MELINDA PRUNTY AND FAMILY OF NATHAN SHEMWELL AT THE CAPITOL IN FRANKFORT, KY

CHIEF RICKY KING

207 N. 2nd Street
Central City, KY 42330
Phone 270-754-2345
Fax 270-754-2493

September 20, 2017

Powderly Holiness Church
c/o Larry Shemwell
36 Phillip Uzzle Lane
Central City KY 42330

Dear Friends:

    I would like to congratulate you and your family on the 50th anniversary since the founding of Powderly Holiness Church. Your joy in this wonderful achievement serves as an inspiration to all of Muhlenberg County.

    The church's longstanding commitment to God and the Muhlenberg County community is to be commended, as well as Pastor Larry Shemwell's 40 years of service. You and all of the members of Powderly Holiness Church have my best wishes as you continue your service and commitment to God and this community.

Sincerely,

Ricky King

Chief Ricky D. King
Central City Fire Dept.

City of Central City

214 North First Street
Central City, KY 42330

BARRY SHAVER, Mayor
DAVID G RHOADES, City Administrator

Telephone 270-754-5097
270-754-2336
FAX 270-754-5745

On behalf of the City of the City of Central City I would like to take this opportunity to congratulate Powderly Holiness Church on their 50th Anniversary. Powderly Holiness Church has been a pillar in the community for half a century and has spread the word of God to many households across Muhlenberg County and beyond. Providing spiritual leadership and at the same time educational opportunities for their children and young people.

Congratulations are also in order for Pastor Larry Shemwell for his dedicated service to the Lord at Powderly Holiness Church for 40 years. Pastor Shemwell has displayed an example to all Christians as to fulfill your calling and use your spiritual gifts given to you by God to bring him glory each and every day.

In today's time, it seems many Churches are closing their doors for various reasons., Pastors are like revolving doors looking for the best opportunity or highest pay. Powderly Holiness Church and Pastor Larry Shemwell have set the example of perseverance and sticking to Gods plan he has had for them.

Once again I say congratulations for these two extraordinary accomplishments and thank you for the service you have provided for our County. The good Lord has truly blessed you and will continue to do so as you move forward and look to celebrate the next milestones ahead.

Respectfully,

Barry Shaver
Mayor

CURTIS MCGEHEE
Muhlenberg County Sheriff
P.O. Box 227 • 100 Main Street • Greenville, KY 42345
Phone (270) 338-3345   Fax (270) 338-0766   Dispatch (270) 338-2000 / 9-1-1

September 25, 2017

Dear Powderly Holiness Church:

I recently learned that you will soon be celebrating 50 years of ministry as Powderly Holiness Church. I would like to commend you for your service for the Lord and for your dedication to our community.

On more than one occasion I have witnessed your church reaching out to others. I have been especially impressed with your love and passion for children. I have also witnessed a loving and warm spirit among the believers in your fellowship.

The Powderly Holiness Church has developed a strong and positive testimony in Muhlenberg County. I personally hold your church in high esteem.

I would also like to express my admiration for your dear pastor. As a child, I once spent the night in the Shemwell's home. From my childhood until this day, I have loved and appreciated your pastor. His ministry in your church and throughout our community is far reaching.

Brother Shemwell, thank you for 40 years of distinguished Christian service and thank you for always being a wonderful example.

I trust that God will continue to bless Powderly Holiness Church and your pastor in your efforts and labor.

Affectionately,

Curtis McGehee

Curtis McGehee

www.ingramcontent.com/pod-product-compliance
Lightning Source LLC
Chambersburg PA
CBHW071610080526
44588CB00010B/1081